Knowle

C000171182

CURRICULUM STUDIES
General Editor: David Jenkins

Curriculum: an introduction
David Jenkins and Marten D. Shipman

Designing the Curriculum
Hugh Sockett

Changing the Curriculum
Barry MacDonald and Rob Walker

Curriculum Evaluation
David Hamilton

Knowledge and Schooling
Richard Pring

Culture and the Classroom
John Reynolds and Malcolm Skilbeck

Knowledge and Schooling

Richard Pring

Open Books

First published in 1976 by Open Books Publishing Limited,
West Compton House, Nr Shepton Mallet, Somerset, England
Reprinted 1978
Reprinted 1980

© Richard Pring 1976
Hardback: ISBN 0 7291 0096 0
Paperback: ISBN 0 7291 0091 X

Filmset in Linotron 11 pt Baskerville by
G. A. Pindar & Son Ltd, Scarborough, N. Yorkshire
Printed in Great Britain by The Pitman Press, Bath

Contents

Editor's introduction

Curriculum studies is one of the growth points in education today. In essence it takes as problematic what should be planned, taught and learned in our schools. It is a central and centralising study organised around the choices facing the practitioner. It can be gritty and ragged about the edges, lacking the settled conceptual apparatus of other disciplines in education, but it aspires to being *usable*. Curriculum studies is a recognition of the needs felt by practitioners for better ways of describing, explaining and justifying what goes on in educational programmes. The question *What ought we to be teaching in our schools?* is a more complex one than appears at first glance: this series explores the underlying complexities.

There are perhaps two major reasons for the present upsurge of interest in curriculum theory and practice. The first is that we have just completed in British education the first cycle of the curriculum reform movement (a cycle brought to an end by the current financial stringency); this movement brought to the surface a number of pressing issues – it was never simply a question of updating the knowledge component. There have been two main trends in the analysis of the 'curriculum reform' phenomenon. The first stresses the movement as an attempt to *institutionalise* the whole process of curriculum change and seeks to explore the full implications of making the curriculum into a legitimate object of social policy. The second points to the 'grass roots' image of reform and characterises the curriculum reform movement in terms of the emergence of 'curriculum entrepreneurs', first-generation project directors who backed hunches derived from their own experience. Both accounts raise problems. The first suggests that the principal issue is a boundary dispute over professional autonomy between administrators and teachers. The second invites us to view the curriculum reform movement as a free enterprise system in which change agents invent and disseminate classroom novelty in the teeth of an inadequate infrastructure for planned change. But neither of these 'social movement' perspectives is much help in generating the kind of research tradition that would allow us to explore the conflicting premisses behind alternative proposals.

The second reason for the upsurge in interest to some extent complements the first. I refer to the emergence of a 'community of discourse' in the universities, in the schools, in the colleges of education and the teachers' centres, which have become seriously interested in curriculum as an area of study. This is not to suggest that the 'practical' reform movement spawned a derivative 'theoretical' literature, for the same people were frequently involved in both. Indeed such an overlap is wholly appropriate given the aspiration of curriculum studies to be a theory about practice – and a practitioners' theory. One sign of the emerging 'community of discourse' has been the proliferation of courses in curriculum, both in-service and as part of initial training.

This series is an attempt to explore the main issues likely to recur in curriculum studies courses. Its authors have all been involved directly in curriculum reform, either as teachers, project members or evaluators. All are familiar with the world of the classroom. Most have many years of teaching experience (in my own case over eight in a South Wales comprehensive school) and all are currently involved in preparing and teaching curriculum studies in teacher education.

Although part of a series, each book is capable of standing on its own. All have end-of-chapter summaries, and suggestions for further reading.

This particular volume, *Knowledge and Schooling*, was written by Richard Pring, who is currently Lecturer in Curriculum Studies at the London Institute of Education, having previously worked at the Cambridge Institute of Education. Dr Pring combines his lecturing and tutorial work with some weekly teaching in an Inner London comprehensive school, and is trying to develop an approach to teacher education that makes school-based work a major focus and grounding for theoretical studies.

Knowledge and Schooling examines several approaches to the place of knowledge in the curriculum: the philosophical arguments for 'forms of knowledge'; the emergent sociology of knowledge; the claims made on behalf of the interest-based curriculum; and Pring's own analysis of 'commonsense knowledge'. *Knowledge and Schooling* is not only a guided tour of these markedly different approaches but a plea that they be considered in relation to the need for a usable practitioners' theory. Indeed the book springs from Dr Pring's own attempts to reconsider existing theories in the light of his experience of teaching.

David Jenkins

INTRODUCTION

This book attempts to develop an idea. The idea was initially a response to the kind of curriculum theory, especially philosophical theory, which tends to prevail at colleges and institutes of education. I felt that in many respects the prevailing theory lacked the philosophical justification necessary for such widespread and unquestioned acceptance. Moreover, there seemed to be a gulf between the theory and the practical wisdom required for the task of educating so many pupils and students of different cultural background and degrees of motivation in so many different contexts. The very variety and complexity of the educational scene seemed to require a more generous approach to the philosophy of the curriculum.

The idea, then, was initially formed in response to an existing theory of practice that was questionable at both a theoretical and a practical level. This book is nothing more than an attempt to articulate that idea, to give it shape, to make it publicly accessible, and thus to reveal to myself, as well as to others, both its strengths and its weaknesses.

In chapters 1 and 2 I look at the prevailing philosophical position and question it. The prevailing position is that education is about the development of mind, that mind is in some sense determined by the growth and the structure of knowledge, that there are logically different kinds of knowledge, and that it is from these different, publicly developed, kinds of knowledge that curriculum content should be drawn. I do not deny all this. Indeed, I agree (and argue in these chapters) that any theory of education must have a theory of mind, and that central to the development of mind is the growth of knowledge. But I also argue that those who currently share this position have too narrow and too neat a view of what that knowledge is, and thus an inadequate concept of mind. This is likely to lead (as it so clearly does in the practice of our schools, colleges and universities) to the neglect of the very minds we are employed to educate.

Chapter 3 examines an opposite position, that of focusing the curriculum, not upon the divisions of knowledge suggested by curriculum philosophers, but upon the active interests of the particular minds to be educated. The 'child-centred' position, rooted in the work and writings of (amongst others) Kilpatrick and Dewey, is so alien to the currently prevailing philosophy that I am persuaded that there must be some truth in it. I try to distil what I believe to be true in what they say, but remain critical of the over-all position.

Caught, then, within the tension between two philosophical positions, I look in chapter 4 for some assistance from one current criticism of the prevailing philosophy, namely, that put forward by some sociologists of knowledge. In a sentence, they argue that knowledge is socially situated and is therefore flexible rather than logically tidy. Their criticism has had impact not only upon theorists but also upon practitioners, who have found in it an attempt to make sense of their practice, which just isn't like the practice that the prevailing theory would like it to be. I feel very sympathetic towards the sociological position. But in many respects it is wrong, and to try to work out why it is wrong is a taxing and rewarding exercise. The strength of their position lies in the emphasis upon the socially constructed and socially situated nature of how we think, and of what counts

2

as knowledge. This is a truth too often neglected in curriculum thinking, and becoming clear about the nature and limitations of this truth provides yet a further stage in the evolution of my argument.

These four chapters are essentially critical of currently held positions in the debate. But each critical piece indicates where I feel the truth to lie, and this I attempt to develop in the remaining chapters. Firstly, in chapter 5, I look at the commonsense knowledge that children bring to school. Isn't it this – undifferentiated and practical, but often very sophisticated – that needs to be educated? But what sense can we make of commonsense language, knowledge, and judgment? I can only show the direction in which my own reflection is going. In chapter 6 I examine the possibility of a more integrated curriculum, developing some of the insights that are contained (confusedly maybe) in its frequent recommendation. Finally chapter 7 seeks to bring these scattered clues together and to outline principles, implicit within my argument, for selecting curriculum content.

The development of knowledge is only part (though a crucial part) of the development of mind and it is this development that the curriculum must be centrally concerned with. But how can we adequately grasp this complex entity we call 'mind'? I do not know. What alone I am certain of is that, however difficult it is to reach a satisfactory answer, anyone seriously engaged in teaching has an answer, and we (each of us) must first begin to examine *that* critically – and hopefully make it accessible to the criticism of others.

1 EDUCATION AND KNOWLEDGE

1. Educability

I was recently asked to teach social studies to fourth formers in an inner London comprehensive school. There was no set syllabus to teach. What I taught therefore was to be of my own devising. The reason why they were to be taught social studies was that the systematic study of society provided a kind of knowledge to which, on a well balanced *educational* programme, pupils should be introduced. Not only was there a *kind* of knowledge about society without which one would remain ignorant of a very important area of experience but also this kind of knowledge needed to be introduced to them systematically. Hence my task in planning a year's work was to analyse what this distinctive kind of knowledge was, to isolate the central and typical features of it, and to get the pupils (by whatever method proved suitable) to grasp these features.

I reflected upon what this distinctive kind of knowledge might be – not an easy task because it was not clear what to look for in picking out a specific kind of knowledge. Is a kind of knowledge (i.e. what gets separate treatment on a well balanced curriculum and thus what pupils are systematically introduced to) identified by an interrelated set of problems that worry people – some people at least, if not the

4

pupils? Or is it identified by a certain kind of method, a way of solving problems or of seeking information? Or is it identified by a theoretical position – a set of interrelated concepts and a body of propositions that are all logically interconnected and that together seek to explain something? Or is it identified by an agreed literature, or simply by what people who are called sociologists, historians or geographers tend to write about? Possibly the answer is a mixture of all of these, and something more besides. There is no neatness in this area and the *sort* of thing one looks for in picking out one kind of knowledge (history, say) may be quite different from the sort of thing one looks for in picking out another (e.g. geography).

Having finally devised a scheme and produced a large number of work cards with 'provocative' social studies problems, key concepts exemplified by 'lively' illustration, and small tasks that would indicate some of the methods and skills of social science, two things happened. The girls used my carefully produced, meticulously devised cards as batons with which to waylay each other; the boys continued to play pontoon and, when confronted with my multicoloured work scheme, told me to fuck off. My objectives remained unsullied on the table.

That then was my curriculum problem – how to survive for the next three terms in a manner that would be reciprocally worthwhile and useful.

This detail of a curriculum failure is important. It forced me to raise curriculum questions in a quite different way. Previously it had been assumed (as it is in so much curriculum literature) that the curriculum should be a systematic initiation into certain kinds of knowledge, and that the content of what is taught should therefore be drawn from those areas. But the rejection of what was offered – whether it was of the particular categories of thought or of the problems that I thought they should be investigating – made me ask more fundamental questions. What was it to educate *these*

5

pupils who, despite their rejection in this and doubtless other classes of the different kinds of knowledge to which they were being systematically introduced, had nonetheless minds that questioned, puzzled, doubted, drew conclusions, made inferences, and so on? And to ask what would count as educating *these* pupils with their ways of thinking, their feelings and emotions, their grasp of physical and social reality, would not necessarily, it seemed to me, find an answer within traditionally conceived kinds of knowledge so neatly outlined by these curriculum theorists. Or, if the answer did lie necessarily along those lines, more convincing reasons would be needed.

Let me expand upon this point. The question 'What is it to educate *these* pupils?' did itself make several assumptions. It assumed that questions about educational worth could not be too far separated from an investigation of, and a concern for, the recipients of that education – the individual people whom I was trying to educate. By this I do not mean a class of people or a hypothetical normal set but the particular individuals. It is Peter's or Mary's way of thinking, reacting, feeling, questioning that is to be educated. And to treat such individuals, diverse as they are in their various mental interests and activities, as a homogenous whole, or to introduce them, despite their differences both in modes of thought and in matters of concern, to a uniform way of thinking conceived without those individuals in mind, would not seem to be an education of *them*.

At this stage I am, as I was in that school, trying to find my way about. The preceding paragraph needs to be qualified. Some readers will have already detected a suspicion of relativism or indeed subjectivism. Surely, they are saying, the different kinds of knowledge that we traditionally teach in schools and colleges are public ways of thinking, legitimate irrespective of the idiosyncratic interests of particular individuals. To educate *them* is to introduce *them* to ways of thinking, standards of conduct, levels of feeling and aspira-

6

tion, the value and validity of which are independent of individual choice or preference. Deny this, they might say, and everything (therefore nothing) is equally valid, everything (therefore nothing) is equally valuable.

With this criticism I in part agree. I wish to go so far with it. But how far is what I am trying to work out. My original statement needs to be qualified, and what follows in this book is really an attempt to provide that qualification. Possibly the way to begin is to examine a second assumption behind my question 'What is it to *educate* these pupils?', namely, that to educate is to help the development or growth of mind, as it is shown through a variety of mental activities: questioning, seeking, explaining, doubting, feeling, hoping, reacting, imagining, fantasising, and so on. It is because children have minds and engage in a wide variety of mental activities which for better or worse can be influenced by others that we have such a concept as education. Behind any educational programme lies a philosophy of mind, both what counts as having a mind and what counts as having it more abundantly.

To talk about the development of mind has, of course, its problems. We seem to be landed with a rather mysterious entity, distinct from the body but acting upon it, with a form of life (spiritual or mental) peculiarly its own. I do not wish here to enter too far into the philosophy of mind, but I believe that many philosophical problems are caused by having nouns (with the apparent function of referring to objects) when adjectives will do just as well. It is quite compatible with our everyday ways of understanding and speaking to see 'mind' as a shorthand form of referring to the many, wide ranging abilities, capacities, tendencies that explain how people act and react and that at the same time seem to escape explanation in purely physical terms. Such qualities are reflected in the mental concepts we daily use – thoughtful, imaginative, creative, intelligent, sensitive, persevering, strong-willed, affectionate, and so on. Educating, as opposed to drilling or conditioning, would seem to be concerned with the development of such mental qualities which constitute the life of the mind.

To say this, of course, answers no problems: it simply indicates a little more clearly what, and how many, our problems are. A moment's reflection will make us aware how difficult it is to get a grip on these concepts, indispensible though they are to our everyday discussion of the people whom we are trying to educate. My task with the fourth formers in this, as in any other teaching situation, was how to make them more thoughtful, imaginative, intelligent, etc, than they were before – for the very fact, not to be forgotten, that they were conscious beings meant that they already had thoughts, images, choices to make, problems to solve, feelings to control, affections, etc. They were already engaged in some form of mental life (even Deborah) and it was *that* that made them educable.

If I am labouring this issue it is because so much follows from this reflection. Firstly, too much stress at the outset upon fixed programmes or syllabuses, upon specific subject-matter to be learnt, upon initiation into this or that kind of knowledge, upon certain highly worked out, publicly legitimated forms of knowledge, carries too clear a notion of success or failure in education. Pupils are labelled as having passed the initiation tests or not, as being educable or not. The impression received (because that is the message given) by so many pupils is that education is not for them, despite the very active mental life that each already is engaged in and despite therefore the very educability of each and every one of them. Too much stress at the outset upon syllabuses and content distracts attention from the individual mental lives that alone give point and sense to educational programmes.

Secondly, focusing attention upon the mental life of those who are to be educated reminds us of the very complexity and variety of those human potentialities to be improved. A child's education must not be narrowly conceived. Too narrow a concern with the growth of knowledge and too

8

narrow a conception of knowledge leaves large parts of that mental life untouched. It fails to educate.

However, there does seem to be a very special connection between the education of these pupils and the growth of knowledge. To know more and to know better does not seem to be just one amongst several kinds of mental activity. It has a privileged place.

There is a widely held view that education is primarily concerned with the development of knowledge, hence the insistence of some that certain kinds of knowledge (publicly accepted) are to be learnt, and the criticism of others that education is reduced to the selling of a commodity that neglects the needs of the individual. I wish to subscribe to the view that education is primarily concerned with the development of knowledge so long as a sufficiently generous analysis of knowledge is accepted. My insistence upon such generosity is not entirely idiosyncratic, nor is it being prescriptive. Brief attention to how the word is used will reveal how rich it is in its application.

The major point that I want to make, then, is that in educating we are concerned with the development, indeed enrichment, of mental life, and that central to such development is the growth of knowledge. But in making this point I shall be insisting upon an analysis of knowledge that does justice to the manifold way in which people in general, and these pupils in particular, are consciously engaged in a number of activities.

2. Mental achievement and conceptual development

However slow and ineducable the pupils may seem, they have already achieved a fairly sophisticated knowledge that is essential to the various mental activities in which they engage. To have emotions, to find their way about, to be aware of other objects and people, to be aware of themselves, to think, to muse, or to ponder, is already to have mastered a complex conceptual map of the world. It is already to have learnt a wide range of concepts.

The mastery of these concepts is in part an individual achievement (a way of dividing up and classifying *their* experience and of picking out individual objects within it), but it is also in part a public and social activity in that they have achieved a system of reference and of classification which has been developed by other people and given a permanence in language more enduring than the achievements of any one individual. By learning a language one learns a particular way of looking at the world – of classifying and identifying things, of discriminating between events, and indeed of gaining mastery over them, and to acquire a more refined and extensive set of concepts is to develop a capacity for greater discrimination within experience, a more sensitive and extensive awareness. Central to any educative activity must be greater discrimination following upon the acquisition of a more refined and extensive conceptual structure. Another way of making the same point is to say that some thinking is basic to any mental activity whatsoever, and that concepts are the necessary tools of thought. To acquire concepts is to acquire the capacity to think; to acquire different kinds, as well as a wide range, of concepts is to acquire the power to think more effectively.

It is necessary to define clearly exactly what one means by a concept. To say that it is some principle of unity in one's experience is a useful provisional definition, but one that leaves a lot to be explained. Examples might indicate what I mean. To have a concept of 'red' is to be able to bring lots of experiences, separate in both time and space, together because of some features that these experiences have in common. To have a concept of 'house' is again to see some common feature in a whole range of otherwise distinct experiences. But note the differences in these two examples. In the first case, the unifying factor or principle is a sensible quality, red; in the second example, the unifying principle is the use to which different objects are put. Conceptual development lies not simply in increasing the number of concepts that the pupil has (i.e. in increasing the number of unifying principles applied to experience) but also in extending the kinds of unifying principles. The very young child will tend to conceptualise things according to affective characteristics – how things affect him (what is enjoyable to eat or what is frightening). Later, and very rapidly, he will come also to classify things according to sensible characteristics (e.g. colours or shapes).

It is interesting to observe the slow acquisition of language by a small child. The gradual mastery of colour concepts, for example, is not simply a matter of memorising names which are to be attached to certain visual phenomena; it is a matter also of acquiring certain rules for classifying experience in one way rather than another. Point to a red spot, saying 'red', and the two-year-old will not know what sort of thing you are picking out. He will not yet have got the rules of the colour game – the kind of principle of unity which he is being expected to apply. Again, the meaning of the word 'because' is mastered slowly by the young child, because of the rather different conceptual connections it picks out. To conceptualise things according to cause and effect (which is one function that the word 'because' has) is not something that a very young child can do. Even when he uses the word, it is possible to detect that he is not using it in the same way that an adult uses it. He hasn't got their concept, say, of cause and effect. He has therefore not acquired at a very fundamental level the very tools of thought that the adult has, and part of educating that child will be to enable him to use concepts in that way.

To have a concept then is to have some principle of unity in one's experience, but such a principle involves also knowing how one concept interconnects with others. To have a concept of 'mother' is also to have a concept of 'father', 'son', 'daughter', etc. The definition of any one of these con-

11

cepts makes a reference to the others and the gradual acquisition of a concept consists partly in learning its definition, its interconnections. A young child who understands by 'daddy' any relatively friendly man has still further connections to make before she has the same concept that I (as a daddy) have. And I, understanding by 'acid' a substance that is sour, causes chemical reaction upon other substances, and turns litmus paper red, have not quite the same concept as a chemist whose definition of the concept would be more precise and far-reaching in its interconnections. Indeed a great deal of philosophical work consists in tracing these interconnections, the idea being that to understand a concept is to understand how people view a particular segment of their experience, the values attached to it, the underlying beliefs, the assumptions they make.

The main significance of Piaget's work is his analysis of the logic of children's thinking which shows that at different stages of growth children are able to conceptualise in some ways but not in others. That is, they can only bring a limited number of principles of unity to their experience. Children develop early a capacity to tie phenomena (otherwise distinct both in time and in space) together in the concept of an 'object', external to and independent of the knowing subject. Only later will the child have the kinds of concepts that will enable him to connect together such objects according to principles of cause and effect. Even though the acquisition of concepts is essential to the extension of the powers and activity of the mind, it is of little use trying to teach a child those concepts which employ a principle of unity beyond the mode of his current conceptual thinking. For example, there seems little point in teaching a child the abstractions of scientific theory whilst the logic of his thinking is still within a conceptual framework dominated by what Piaget calls 'concrete operations'. When, however, basic rules or principles of unity in experience have been learnt (e.g. in relation to colour), then *that* particular area of his conceptual 'map' can

12

become more refined, ever more discriminating. The development of language, of colour language for example, necessarily involves the development of concepts.

By learning a language therefore one learns to organise experience in a variety of ways that others have found, and are still finding, adequate and useful for a variety of different purposes. Possibly the best way to acquire a language is to talk to other people, gradually mastering through communication with them the meanings that inform their discourse. Not understanding what a person says may be due to a variety of factors, carelessness of diction, sloppiness in the use of words, but it may be due simply to not knowing what words mean – to not having a particular concept or to not seeing things in a certain way. But how else are pupils to be helped to overcome their own inadequate grasp of publicly available concepts other than through being encouraged to engage in conversation – a conversation which will constantly fail in its purpose unless enhanced at the right moment with appropriate concepts. These concepts, offered as explanatory tools, will in all probability be provided by the teacher. And yet the curriculum of our schools is often constructed in a way that makes conversation impossible: the system of short periods in which a different teacher is related to in a formally arranged environment with minimum attention given to basic conditions of social interaction.

Immediately after writing the paragraph above I took the fourth form social studies group to the Houses of Parliament where they were shown around by their M.P. The *educational* value of such visits is never easy to assess. How can one know the consequences of such an experience upon the mental life of sixteen adolescents who, in their separate ways and with varying degrees of interest, observed, paid attention to, and participated in what was going on? The consequences would depend on what they understood, but what they understood would itself depend on what they were attending to and what

13

previous understandings they had. The value of this visit lay in the more intensive conversation it opened up, a conversation that showed that the pupils had inadequate concepts, had failed to understand, and needed tools of thought at too elementary a level to warrant a special course called 'politics' or 'social studies'. Both the diagnosis of such needs and the continuing attempt to meet them required intelligent, sensitive teaching from a generally educated person. The difficulties could not be foreseen and hence the outcome could not be precisely preconceived or planned for. A curriculum need not have precise objectives despite the theory which tells us otherwise.

Throughout his education the pupil becomes increasingly familiar with adult concepts (the publicly accepted concepts mediated by the school). These differ from his (the pupil's) in that they are more complex, more demanding in definition and application, and provide a more refined and more adequate picture of the world for a larger number of purposes. In acquiring those concepts the pupil will frequently proceed by trial and error. He will go wrong; he will fail to communicate or to understand. His faltering attempts to convey meaning or to understand might be likened to the slow testing of hypotheses: frequent failure requiring frequent readjustment, reformulation. Eventually the suggested reformulation of how things are receives confirmation; it is verified in successful communication. But the whole struggle to find and reach agreement on meaning is essentially an achievement – the mastery after frequent failure of a particular way of describing and accounting for experience. And to talk of achievement is to introduce the notion of standards – of succeeding, of coming up to scratch, of performing adequately.

This involves a paradox which will constantly recur throughout the book. What we learn by learning a language is one way of looking at the world. Language is both socially developed and socially situated. The teacher at different levels of schooling and through different specialist studies is providing what is, in his view, a better way of organising experience. Nonetheless, it remains but one way. One can never say 'This is *the* way' or 'This is *the* concept'. Hence in helping a child to acquire concepts, we are teaching him to attain what has been formed by others. We are teaching him the adult's or the specialist's way of organising experience, not *the* way. Even the young child, in lumping together all towered buildings as churches or in seeing all events as the product of magical forces, has *a* way of conceiving the world, although it is not that of grown-ups. The adolescent may have a range of concepts whereby events and objects are linked together differently from those of the teacher. His conceptual map is different, but one cannot say that it is wrong. This brings us face to face with our paradox, for, in talking about the development of the child's mind I am insisting upon the acquisition and refinement of others' concepts whilst at the same time pointing out the conventional nature of those concepts. One of the difficulties to face in the philosophy of the curriculum is to reconcile the importance of the public definitions of conceptual structure, to which the pupil is being asked to submit, with the legitimate individual deviations from that structure and the possibility of his contributing to it.

I argue therefore that central to the development of mental life is the acquisition of an ever more discriminating conceptual map of the physical and social world. It is through a language that a child is offered a rich and complex way of organising experience. It gives the individual not only a detached understanding of the world, but some purchase on it, and a capacity to bend it to his purposes. There are specialist languages which give access to a specialist kind of knowledge, and the layman may not have been initiated into these languages. He will not have those particular concepts that enable him to organise his experience and his activity in that rather special kind of way. For example, without a grasp

15

of such precisely defined and interconnected concepts as 'molecule', 'electron', 'neutron', 'atom', etc, a whole way of ordering and explaining experience is denied him.

Possibly one of the most important questions for the secondary school curriculum concerns the extent to which the development of mind (the increase in its powers, the extension and improvement of its activities) requires the initiation into such specialist languages. My own view (developed in chapter 2) is that an exaggerated importance has been given to them and that this has resulted in miseducation in many cases.

3. Knowing how and knowing that

A number of mental states, activities, and achievements have in common an act of judgment whereby concepts are applied to experience, objects are identified and classified for particular purposes, events are explained by certain principles, or otherwise distinct objects and events are connected. Even being conscious or aware requires a consciousness or awareness of something, and this implies the application of concepts. Admittedly one needs as a teacher to distinguish between different kinds of mental activity but, whatever these distinctions, there is a common judgmental element in which concepts are applied and standards are submitted to. Education must be concerned with the acquisition and proper use of concepts and with the respect for, and submission to, standards.

In pursuing this point it is important to distinguish between different kinds of knowing. Philosophers (and teachers) have concentrated their attention upon knowledge claims in the sense of 'knowing that' – 'I know that $100 \times 5 = 500$', '. . . that acid turns litmus paper red', '. . . that murder is wrong'. But knowledge is understood here to be more than a mental state (i.e. a strong belief or a facility to pop the right answer out at the right moment).

That more is, firstly, that what is believed is in fact true and, secondly, that in so believing one has good grounds for believing it to be true. What might be called both the necessary and the sufficient conditions for knowing that something is the case can be set out as follows (where p stands for any proposition):

I know that p = (i) I believe that p
              (ii) p is true
              (iii) There are good grounds for
                   believing p to be true.

The first condition requires amongst other things that I understand the concepts employed in the proposition p and know how and when to apply them. The second condition however requires not just my understanding, not just a psychological state of mind (a strong conviction, say), but something about the world that is independent of my wanting or wishing it. Beliefs need to be tempered by reality in order to be knowledge. If I claim to know that Johnny was the thief and then have it proved to me that he was not, I have to withdraw my claim that I know. To have therefore a theory about the development of mind (to have an educational theory) is also to have some general view of truth – or what it means to say that what I believe is an adequate or a correct account of reality. What conditions existing independently of my particular conviction would make my statement correct?

The third condition is an attempt to distinguish knowledge from what otherwise might be merely true belief, as when I believe truly that, for example, Red Rush will win the 4.30, but do so as a result of guesswork, prejudice, invalid argument or reliance upon unreliable authority. The significance of this for my purposes is the further insistence upon standards – here, the criteria by which one accepts the validity of a person's claim. Indeed this is an extension of the second condition. For just as a proposition is true or false in that it *correctly* says what is the case, so a *claim* that a proposition is true is valid or not depending on whether the grounds for saying it is true are *appropriate* ones.

Hence the curriculum, in so far as it is concerned with the development of mind, must seek not only a continual development of the conceptual structures through which experience is organised and knowledge claims are formulated, but also the mastery of those standards of reasoning or argument or judgement which make the grounds for one's beliefs good ones. Knowledge is an achievement, frequently to be gained (as the mastery of anything is to be gained) only after continued struggle and risk of failure. And, as with the mastery of anything, it requires all too often a disciplined approach and an openness to constant correction and redirection.

This general analysis of knowledge, in terms of the acquisition and use of certain sets of concepts and the submission to standards (of argument, performance, etc) is unaffected by there being different kinds of knowledge. An important distinction is made between 'knowing that' (which I have just examined) and 'knowing how' – between belief-type and procedural-type knowledge. Whether or not John knows *how* to solve a problem depends partly upon the merits of his public performance, not on the truth of what he says. Does he perform intelligently, shrewdly, wisely, as opposed to stupidly, indiscriminately, shortsightedly? To learn *how* to do something is an achievement that involves an adequate conceptualisation of the problem certainly, but also coming up to scratch in one's *performance*.

The distinction between 'knowing that' and 'knowing how' is worth dwelling on a little. So much of school curriculum is concerned with 'knowing that', being able to make correct statements backed up with appropriate reasons, and yet so often primacy ought to be given to procedural knowledge or 'knowing how'. A very young child knows *how* to speak grammatically without knowing *that* 'to form the plural you add "s"', etc, etc. Most people know *how* to

18

deduce a conclusion from premisses without knowing *that* 'In the syllogistic mode of reasoning the middle term must be distributed at least once.' A child knows *how* to balance on a bicycle without being able to repeat the laws of mechanics.

Furthermore 'learning that' is not necessarily the best way to 'learn how'. The theory of making friends or of social success will not necessarily teach one *how* to make friends or *how* to gain ease in social relationships. One learns how to speak grammatically and logically, how to ride a bicycle, how to make friends and succeed in social relationships, by trying to *do* these things (not by talking about them or learning the theory of them). And in trying to *do* one is open to corrction, to adjustment, to advice – one submits in one's practice to the criticism of others.

I feel that the neglect of this distinction is responsible for so much dead weight in the curriculum. We are so concerned with 'knowing that' (possibly because of the greater ease with which it can be examined on a large scale) that we forget that much of this kind of knowledge is a very sophisticated reflection upon 'knowing how', an attempt to make explicit and put into statements the principles that are already operating in successful practice. Knowledge communicated through statements (as in lectures and textbooks) often arises from systematic reflection upon the practical know-how which is being theorised about. Certainly in many cases the validity of the theory lies in the degree to which it improves a person's practice or his knowledge *how* to perform. And yet so much knowledge is taught in total disconnection from the practical world which gives it point. Educational theory is generally divorced from educational practice; it becomes a body of theory that 'takes off' from (is developed, debated about, agreed or disagreed upon without systematic reference to) the practice, the knowing how, about which it is theorising.

I have recently been involved in developing a Mode III Certificate of Secondary Education (C.S.E.) examination in community service. Much that we wanted to have examined, and thus to be the basis of assessment, was rejected because the C.S.E. is awarded (so we were told) for the development of knowledge, and knowledge is the sort of thing that can be written down on paper. I agreed that the certificate should assess knowledge (knowledge is central to the development of mind, which is what education is concerned with) but disagreed that knowledge (even the most important kind of knowledge) is necessarily what can be written down. I have known able car mechanics who know *how* to take engines to pieces, diagnose and correct faults in most imaginative ways, reassemble the parts, and yet be almost illiterate. Many are the people who know *how* to be sensitive (and this involves thought, reflection, imagination) without being able to express in the form of statements (i.e. as knowledge that . . .) what they are doing or what is the secret of their success. Hence it seems a perfectly legitimate aspiration on the part of school to award C.S.E. for success in the various community service activities without insisting upon much written evidence of knowledge. The C.S.E. Board simply needs to distinguish between 'knowing that' and 'knowing how', and to treat the latter with greater respect.

4. Mental qualities

Whatever the differences in kinds of knowledge, the development of these does seem to require certain mental qualities that can be characterised in a fairly general way and that should be continually fostered through the curriculum. They could be called 'intellectual virtues' and it is with a consideration of these that I would like to conclude this chapter.

I have referred to the mastery of, and submission to, standards, whether in one's performance, or in one's various claims to knowledge. Such mastery of and submission to standards implies both the possibility of improvement and the possibility of failure. There is no limit to be set upon such improvement, nor can one ever be certain of success. Knowledge must never be confused with certainty. Hence, however learned a person is, he has no reason to absolve himself from the criticism of others. Indeed one mark of the search for excellence and truth is the seeking out of criticism and counterevidence. The strength of one's beliefs lies in their capacity to withstand the criticism of others, and the excellence of one's performance can in part be measured by the acclaim of those who understand the kind of activity one is engaged in. The closed mind – the mind that is satisfied and certain in its own knowledge and know-how – lacks a quality which is crucial to its further education, no matter how learned, well read, and clever the person is. Openness to criticism, and respect for other people as the possible source of criticism, is the first of the intellectual virtues to be fostered through the curriculum.

Connected with openness of mind is a concern for truth – for accuracy in observing, for precision in reporting, for proportioning conclusion to evidence. A clever mind can regularly cook the books, but not an educated one. But a concern for truth is more than a refusal to tell lies. It seeks out the truth, is disciplined in its search for a solution. The disciplined pursuit of the truth – learning and respecting the rules of accurate observation and recording, refusing to rest in the easy and unjustified answer – is a second quality of mind that an educative curriculum will seek to foster.

Thirdly, the reference points of the activities that one engages in are social – social both in criteria for success and in their possible value to other people. Knowledge is so often treated, as the sociologists are fond of telling us, as a commodity, something to be acquired by an individual and used (swapped, sold, bargained with) for all sorts of non-educational purposes. But, however it is treated, knowledge and know-how are not essentially commodities; rather they are individual attainments of socially developed modes of

21

thinking and operating. Their acquisition lies in the introduction to a form of social life and their legitimacy lies in their capacity to withstand social criticism. The essentially social nature of our mental achievements – in their legitimacy, attainment, and maintenance – requires an attitude towards learning which is essentially cooperative rather than competitive. Knowledge is one commodity (if that is the dreadful word to be used) which is never exhausted by mass consumption. Rather should it be advanced by increased participation.

Finally, the extent and complexity of human achievement, in each of the disciplined pursuits on offer, warrants a certain awe, a certain feeling of inadequacy concerning one's own puny efforts. The clever critic of religion, who has no sense of the mystery which provokes the attempt to give a religious account, misses the point – his mind, with all its cleverness, is closed. The humanist, who finds no interest in the technological know-how of his colleague, is similarly cut off without understanding from a wealth of human achievements. And so we might go on. The mark of an educated man is the sense almost of urgency at realising the amount he does not know or the range of activities not yet attempted, let alone mastered.

Hence, the curriculum that is primarily geared to the development of mind will foster certain general qualities which are not the property of any one subject or limited range of activities. I would include amongst such qualities an openness of mind, a concern for the truth, a collaborative spirit, and a sense of humility before the achievements of mankind, whether they be artisitic, literary, technological, moral or religious. Furthermore I believe that such qualities can be fostered to some extent at any age, though I doubt whether they can be so operationalised as to become the precisely planned outcomes of our rational curriculum planners.

Summary

1, 2 Education is concerned with the improvement of the individual mind. This requires both a respect for the particular individual (how *he* is thinking) and a theory of mind – what it is and how to have it more abundantly. Central to the development of mind is the growth of knowledge, and central to this is the refinement and extension of the conceptual framework through which experience is organised. There is a difficulty however which needs to be resolved. The learner is an individual with a particular way of organising *his* experience, whilst the conceptual structures we seek to introduce him to are of others' making. Why should improvement of mind lie in mastering the adult's way of seeing things?

3 Although the development of knowledge is central to the improvement of mind, one must retain a generous definition of knowledge, not confining it to propositional knowledge. Practical knowledge or know-how is of equal significance. Indeed, 'knowledge that' generally presupposes 'knowledge how', and arises from a systematic reflection upon it.

4 Finally the development of mind requires the fostering of certain qualities and powers of the mind which need not be confined to (and thus exclusively developed through) particular types of knowledge.

Further reading

For a detailed analysis of 'education' and its conceptual connection with 'knowledge', read Peters (1966) chapters 1 and 2. Dewey (1916), especially chapters 1 to 5, similarly connects 'education' with both 'knowledge' and 'growth', but there is greater emphasis upon a more pragmatic theory of knowledge, meeting the individual's practical needs. A general, though difficult introduction to the philosophy of knowledge is Hamlyn (1970), especially chapters 2, 3 and 5. An introduction aimed more at educational problems is

Scheffler (1965). The distinction between 'knowing that' and 'knowing how' is made in both these books, but for detailed analysis see Ryle (1949) chapter 2. Bruner (1966) distinguishes between different ways in which we 'represent' experience – through our practical activity, imaginings, and our symbolising them in language. For an introduction to the philosophy of mind read White (1967), especially chapter 2.

2 THE DIFFERENTIATION OF KNOWLEDGE

1. Disciplines

I have already referred to the *disciplined* pursuit of the truth, or the *disciplined* mastery of some activity. This way of expressing it is crucial to my argument, but it needs explaining and expanding upon.

We commonly talk about 'the disciplines', meaning well organised areas of study to which at school or in institutions of higher education we introduce students. But this readiness to use nouns where adjectives will do does tend to mislead us – to make an object out of an activity. 'Disciplines' are disciplined ways of setting about various tasks, and to master a discipline is not to learn or to memorise something that is stable and fixed. Rather it is a matter of learning *how* to do something, to solve a problem, to create something of value, or to produce what is wanted.

'Discipline' is logically connected with following or submitting to rules. A disciplined class conforms to the rules that prescribe how its members should behave (whatever their motives for doing so). Self-discipline implies a submission to rules because one sees their point. Disciplined behaviour, moreover, verges on the habitual. The self-disciplined person like the man of virtue has acquired the habit of proceeding in a certain way – he habitually looks at things, and proceeds, in accordance with the appropriate norms.

It is therefore clear why one refers to 'intellectual disciplines' and to particular people as having mastered them. The scientist knows how to organise material, make observations, test conclusions in ways that constitute a particular tradition in science. The rules of procedure (possibly only implicit in what he and other scientists do) are not simply propositions to be memorised and repeated; they express ways of behaving that have been developed by groups of people, that can be learnt, and that can be followed with greater or lesser skill, more or less habitually, with varying degrees of fidelity.

To learn how to talk is to master the very complex rules of grammar and syntax that prescribe how words are to be formed and put together. To communicate requires the disciplining of one's sounds to rules, and these are mastered by the pupil through imitation, and through correction from parents and teacher.

To argue effectively requires the disciplining of one's words (and one's emotions) to the rules of logic. But to master such rules, to conform one's activities to them, does not require the explicit formulation or acknowledgement of those rules. Children learn to speak grammatically without explicitly knowing or even being able to recognise the rules of grammar. The adult is able to be logical without being able to repeat the rules of the syllogism.

To learn history or other school subjects is as much a matter of learning *how* to do things as learning *that* something is the case. Otherwise history, etc, become simply a matter of learning the products of other people's activity, and the products, totally disconnected from the kinds of activity that produced them, become so many discrete facts to be learnt. They are not seen as the product of the particular selective, analytic, sifting activity of the practitioner. Or, again, to learn philosophy is to participate in the activity of philosophising – to submit oneself to the criticism and the systematic questioning of others, and gradually to master the rules by which the cut and thrust of philosophical argument becomes most effective and enlightening.

The implication of what I am saying is that learning (and in particular initiation into a way of thinking) should be seen much more as a kind of apprenticeship than it normally is – learning how to do something by working alongside the successful practitioner, by imitating, by subjecting oneself to correction and to direction. The rules of activities that scientists or historians or philosophers typically engage in may be picked up and mastered more easily by working alongside the practitioners and by sharing in what they are trying to do. To appreciate the various achievements in such areas of activity requires long apprenticeships, during which one only gradually learns how to proceed. Such appreciation is gained only from a long, rigorous, and practical attempt to understand.

The rules to which the disciplined man submits can be of a very general kind. There are general rules of rational enquiry: for example, taking account of others' objections, and not accepting inconsistencies. One mark of the educated man is that he submits himself to such rules. He is disciplined by the rules of rational behaviour, for these are intimately connected with what it means to have a mind and to exercise it more effectively. But rules may also be specific to particular enquiries or interests. Indeed the history of thought reveals increasingly differentiated traditions of enquiry and activity characterised by ways of identifying problems, of organising experience, of proceeding with experiment or argument, of setting out and communicating the results of one's activity, and so on. These disciplined modes of enquiry were developed within communities of discourse and are transmitted to, and shared with, each new generation. It is the nature of skills once developed that they can in principle be taught to others. Hence we inherit in the culture more or less explicitly socially-developed and publicly-accessible disciplined modes of acting and enquiring. And the essential

27

features of such disciplines — their distinguishing structure – provides the subject-matter from which the teacher can, and must, draw upon in developing the minds of his pupils.

2. Subject-matter and structure

More needs to be said at this stage about the different subject-matters from which the curriculum draws and in which the teacher finds his own expertise and authority. A subject-matter is a way of knowing that is publicly accessible. As a *way* of knowing there must be something about it that distinguishes it from other ways of knowing – a distinct structuring of activity. As a way of *knowing* it requires both concepts and procedures that can be learnt and employed with varying degrees of success. And as something that is *publicly accessible* it must be relatively stable, very likely with an established and possibly formulated set of procedures, developed by and shared with other people. Research into cancer, pop culture in art, the style and technique of cricket, the critical appreciation of Shakespeare's plays, the examination of contemporary institutions, all provide subject-matters which can be drawn upon to extend and refine further the life of the mind – the capacity to think, reflect, make choices, evaluate, criticise. What makes them distinct subject-matters is that each constitutes a socially developed and accessible way of engaging in certain activities, of tackling certain problems in a disciplined way, which can be acquired by others, which sets standards to be striven for, and which can itself be developed and improved by those who have acquired it.

This however may seem too vague and general for most readers. What is it to *structure* activity, and thereby to enable the pursuit of that activity in a disciplined way? What does it mean to talk of structuring the mind?

The characterisation of a disciplined way of thinking (or enquiring or acting) in terms of structure, and of the differ-

28

ences between such disciplines, and their subject-matter in terms of different structures, is now part of curriculum language. Bruner (1960) argues that by introducing pupils to various structures of thinking you introduce them to the 'basic ideas that lie at the heart of all science and mathematics and the basic themes that give form to life and literature', and that these are 'as simple as they are powerful'. Furthermore 'to be . . . in command of these basic ideas, to use them effectively requires a continual deepening of one's understanding of them that comes from learning to use them in progressively more complex forms'. This, in essence, is Bruner's notion of 'the spiral curriculum'. A spiral curriculum is one in which the central, organising ideas (principles, concepts) of a way of thinking are continually presented to the learner but at a level of understanding and of complexity that takes proper account of his stage of development. The development of understanding within this particular activity requires the continual return to these central ideas, the continual attempt to understand their operation and indeed to make them operate in one's own thinking. Such continual attempts should result in a more reflective and abstract mastery over those ideas – a capacity to formulate them and make them explicit, and to see their relevance even when abstracted from concrete situations. A curriculum as it develops should revisit these basic ideas repeatedly, building upon them until the student has grasped the full formal apparatus that goes with them.

Hence Bruner would characterise different kinds of enquiry by basic ideas – concepts and principles. To enter into a disciplined approach to an activity or to a way of thinking about certain problems requires very often the mastery of such ideas or principles; otherwise one would be ignoring the accumulated achievements of man by which such problems have been identified and tackled and mental resources built up and put at our disposal. It is the teacher's task on this view to know what are, in the various activities

29

that might be encouraged, the structuring ideas and procedures, and to ensure that (at whatever level is suitable for the pupil) they are mastered by him. Bruner gives as an example of what he means the principle of leverage in mechanics. The very young child learns how, when it is before him, to operate a see-saw. Later he will show, through variations in position, that he has a working knowledge of general principles of balance and leverage. Later still he will be able to think about this not only through his acting upon the see-saw, but imaginatively, translating this know-how into quite different situations. At a much later stage he may be able to formulate these principles and express them in a very abstract, indeed mathematical form. But this later stage of explicit formulation, or of abstraction from the concrete, is the 'know that' resulting from reflection upon the 'know how' which, at different levels, one has succeeded in mastering in a very concrete and practical way.

However, we could be misled by Bruner's account if we understand it as a statement about what *in general* is meant by the structure of a disciplined activity or a way of thinking. There are different kinds of achievement and they do not all share the same features. I shall pick out four features of a *structured* activity. Rarely will all features be present in any one case. Structure is not so neat a concept.

(a) *Central organising concepts*

To think at all, even at the most elementary, commonsense level, requires the acquisition and use of concepts. But sometimes, in order to be more precise in tackling certain problems or in postulating some theoretical model for explaining what happens, concepts are either invented or are defined more technically and more narrowly than their normal usage would justify. Furthermore such invented or technically defined concepts will be so logically interrelated that the theory can generally be set out in a deductive form. For example, in physics the concepts of 'atom', 'particle', 'element', 'electron', are so tightly interrelated that the theoretical model into which they enter can be set out in deductive, and indeed, mathematical form. The social sciences, in emulating the physical, strive after a more technically defined set of concepts than we normally employ in talking about social life (for example, 'culture', 'role', 'class', 'social group') but there is not the precision or the system that enables the postulation of theoretical models of the kind found in the physical sciences.

(b) *Principles of procedure*
There are many structured activities (socially developed ways of thinking that need to be mastered) where the structure depends not at all upon specifying such constellations of concepts – for example, the various activities which seem to be the special province of historians or philosophers.

The sort of things that historians, literary critics, and philosophers (for example) do require no central concepts or theoretical models. At the same time such activities may be distinguished by general rules of criticism, of sifting evidence, of identifying and tackling kinds of problem. These activities will take place against a background of thought, criticism, and reflection. One learns to be a philosopher from engaging with other philosophers, and one can learn how to do this (as with literary criticism or historical enquiry) without necessarily knowing that the rules for properly engaging in these activities are such and such. Possibly the best way to teach people how to be historians or appreciators of art or philosophers is to do some history, to appreciate some literature, to engage in philosophical argument with them. (Stop talking about how to appreciate Wordsworth and get on with appreciating him.) Of course, not all ways of proceeding are quite so difficult to analyse. The ways of gathering evidence, of setting up and documenting experiments, of sampling, of promulgating one's findings, are probably more clearly understood and more explicitly developed

31

in scientific activities. Courses on method make more sense here and in the behavioural sciences than they would do in philosophy or art appreciation.

It is as well, however, to dwell on the difficulty met very often in formulating and following rules which prescribe how to proceed. To write a poem or an essay or a novel, to paint a landscape or to sculpt a figure is indeed to be disciplined by rules and by one's materials – not anything goes or can go. And yet such rules, hardly discernible, hardly open to formulation, do not determine how to proceed in any detail. Moreover, progress is often made, difficulties overcome, by breaking the rules. But such rule breaking is not arbitrary: it is defensible or not in terms of the work as a whole, of the effect that is created. The point is that the literary or artistic effect and meaning cannot be isolated from the literary and artistic background, from understood conventions against which the piece of work is seen to be literary or artistic. And this must be true, however vague and ill-formulated those rules and conventions are and however much one refuses to be shackled by them. In writing this book I am being disciplined by a range of considerations – integrity to a few basic ideas (possibly only intimations of ideas) which I am trying to work out and make sense of, coherence between the different parts, relevance to possible educational practice, reference to prevailing arguments, etc. Often the failure to be properly disciplined in one's activity can only be intuited. Constantly one returns to correct the writing because it doesn't 'ring quite right'. Doubtless in a few years one will look at it with embarrassment. One will have moved on. Isn't this the case with the artistic or literary or musical attempts of children? They can look back at what they have done, realising that it does not meet the criteria for a well conducted activity or enquiry or account, without being able to say exactly why. They are successfully learning to know *how* without the knowledge *that* which would enable them to explain.

32

(c)   *Criteria of success*

Part of the structure of an activity (what gives it identity and form) is the implicit reference to certain standards which such an activity seeks to come up to. Maybe this is so tightly connected with the preceding sub-section that it does not need separate treatment but, even if that be the case, no harm will come from developing it.

Some pick out as one criterion for a form of knowledge its tests for truth. Personally, I find such a criterion not only to be restrictive but (as I indicated in distinguishing procedural from theoretical knowledge) also to enforce a rather distorted view of the significance of an activity – what it means. To attribute truth or falsity to a statement, argument, or theory is to evaluate it in a particular way, it is, if you like, putting upon it the stamp of success. But there are other achievements where success lies not in being true but in performing well or effectively or conforming to certain rules. Thus an artist may successfully do what he sets out to do, and he may achieve public recognition and acclaim, without his work of art having to be seen as a statement or an argument which would be appropriately called true or false.

In playing games, in participating in community service, in cooking, working in wood, painting, debating, organising an exhibition, the pupils are engaging in activities which have built in criteria of excellence and which therefore provide scope for improvement, mastery, and the sense of achievement. Unless this were the case they could not be educational activities.

Criteria of truth (particular kinds of success criteria or particular kinds of standards whereby we measure or assess enquiries and certain thinking activities) do themselves vary. The truth of moral arguments is not assessed in the same way as the truth of religious arguments. But what is to count as a criterion of truth must not be restricted to a very few. Even within what is generally called the moral sphere of enquiry

33

and argument there are different accepted ways of assessing the truth of what is said: respect for honesty and individual dignity, for the promotion of happiness and avoidance of pain, for integrity, and so on. It all depends on the sort of moral argument one is engaged in; there is no simple answer.

(d) *Problems and interests*

What frequently brings people together in a disciplined enquiry or activity is the set of problems that they see to be in need of solution or the shared interests that they wish to pursue. The interest or the problem provides the disciplining framework, the point of relevance. Maybe, too, such problems or interests have been shared by a sufficient number of people that, despite any clear rules of procedure or agreed criteria of truth or success, there has grown up a literature, an accessible tradition which helps in the tackling of that problem or the pursuit of that interest. To educate the mind here would be to familiarise the student with the ways in which others have thought about these things so that they too might pursue the interest to greater depths or cope with the problem more effectively.

So far then I have given several characteristic or defining features of a disciplined activity, resulting in distinctive subject-matters upon which the curriculum might draw. It does not pretend to be comprehensive. Indeed these are initial thoughts, indications of the way in which more detailed analysis must go. But one thing seems clear. There is no limited number of kinds of knowledge from which certain paradigm cases might be extracted as a basis for the balanced curriculum. The ways in which man has come to organise experience, engage in enquiry, pursue different interests are many. The possible subject-matter of the curriculum therefore will embody different problems, ways of proceeding, kinds of value, and will arise from quite different concerns and purposes. There will always be new modes of enquiry arising in response to new needs, and interests. But

34

in so far as these different enquiries and interests are publicly shared and developed, so they will become stable ways of acting, and from these might be drawn teachable subject-matter for the curriculum.

3. The differentiation of knowledge – a reductionist view

There is a strong tendency to reduce the many to the few, the complex to the simple, the various to the uniform. This is not simply desirable; it is the very life of reason. To have a concept is to have a principle of unity. And life would be too difficult to cope with if we could not perceive sameness or similarity, or have unifying threads that bind otherwise unique events together. But although this tendency is a natural and a necessary one, it can lead us to demand greater simplicity than is warranted by the variety of things.

I have indicated the wide variety of disciplined activities that man engages in and that might be taught to pupils. Subject titles such as English or geography name not one activity that might be pursued in a more or less disciplined way, but several. And it is not clear how these various activities might be somehow bound together under one subject title. The English teacher may teach how to parse sentences, spell correctly, appreciate poetry, report accurately, talk expressively. These are many different activities, each requiring different skills and talents and the mastery of different rules of procedure. It is doubtful that they have much in common.

And yet, despite this variety, there is a commonly held view that the manifold nature of man's knowing activity can be reduced to certain fundamental kinds. If this were true, it would certainly help curriculum planning, for then examples of these few kinds could be made the basis of curriculum activity. A few ways of knowing would give access to the wide range of man's intellectual achievement, an intimation of all that is possible.

35

Phenix (1964) is an example of an educational philosopher attempting to reduce the sum of human consciousness to a few major types from which can be derived specific guidance for curriculum content. He argues that what is distinctively human is the power to 'experience meanings'; that there are different kinds of meaning (i.e. we are conscious of things in a variety of ways); and that, since education is concerned with the development of what is distinctively human and thus of the various ways in which we are conscious of things, curriculum content should be drawn from these different structures of meaning. Hence, before organising a curriculum we ought to work out philosophically what these structures are.

In doing this, Phenix aims to reveal 'the most basic categories of thought' or the most fundamental 'realms of meaning'. He believes that there are nine of these (which he then reduces further to six). They are: symbolics (mathematics, language, logic), empirics (the various sciences), ethics, aesthetics, synthetics, morals, history, philosophy, religion. 'The realms thus chartered provide the foundations for all the meanings that enter into human experience . . . they are the pure and archetypal kinds of meaning that determine the quality of every humanly significant experience.' Particular disciplines (for example, botany, literary criticism) are the concrete manifestations of these 'realms of meaning'. In part 1 of his book Phenix explains these realms of meaning; in part 2 he fills in the details – the main structuring concepts within each realm that should provide the content of the curriculum.

I believe, however, that this kind of philosophical analysis is mistaken and does not provide an adequate basis for selecting curriculum content. The achievements of mankind are very many: there are many different ways in which man has come to enquire in a disciplined manner into a wide range of problems; many are the activities through which excellence of performance is sought and recognised. There seems something prima facie absurd in reducing all such activity and achievement to a very few 'basic categories'. It is as though a very narrow framework is being imposed upon the very many things we do, and we are being told to look at and to understand all these through this framework and no other. Any philosopher who seeks to do this would need to give a very detailed philosophical argument to justify these categories and no others, as the most basic ways of organising experience, categories to which every meaningful experience and activity must conform – even though it does not appear to. And yet no such detailed philosophical argument is given. There are no compelling grounds for believing that Phenix has at last discovered the most fundamental structure of human consciousness.

To embark on such a philosophical enterprise would indeed be an ambitious and daunting task. Furthermore it is doubtful whether it would ever be achieved with sufficient agreement amongst other philosophers to provide a sound foundation for working out in detail what ought to be the content of a school's curriculum. It would seem unwise, therefore, in selecting and organising the content of the curriculum to await the successful outcome of philosophical controversy.

There is a more humble start to philosophising about the curriculum, namely, to examine critically, to try to get clearer about, and to assess the value of the many activities already competing for attention on the curriculum. These are many, and furthermore the kinds of reasons put forward for having them on the curriculum are many – some to do with the pleasure they give, others to do with the usefulness they possess, yet others because they help solve problems of personal or social significance.

A philosopher of education who shares with Phenix the view that a philosophical analysis of knowledge is a prerequisite of curriculum planning is Professor Hirst. According to Hirst (1965) 'a liberal education can only be planned if distinctions in forms of knowledge are clearly understood'.

Since this philosophical belief has had considerable impact upon curriculum theory, and yet runs counter to what I argue in this book, I shall examine it in some detail. Hirst's argument is roughly as follows:

(i) Education is about the development of mind.

(ii) 'Mind' is logically determined by 'knowledge', and 'to acquire knowledge . . . is to have mind in a fuller sense'.

(iii) Knowledge lies in the structuring of experience by concepts and the accompanying criteria of objectivity (in applying those concepts, making inferences, etc).

(iv) In so far as there are (1) logically different kinds of concepts, (2) different criteria of objectivity, (3) distinctive methods for further structuring experience, knowledge is differentiated into (seven) fundamentally distinct forms (tentatively, these are: mathematics, science, morals, aesthetics, religion, human sciences, history).

(v) The formal characteristics of each kind of knowledge must (logically) be respected in the articulation of curriculum objectives, i.e. 'a scheme of education principally governed by the distinctions between the various forms of knowledge'.

Let us first see where Hirst's position is similar to that outlined in this book. First, he sees that central to educational questions is a philosophy of mind – a fundamental view about what it is to have a mind and to have more of it. Secondly, he argues that central to the development of mind is the development of knowledge. Thirdly, he recognises the diversity in kinds of knowledge, and thus attempts to spell out what this diversity consists of.

Where Hirst and I part company is, firstly, in the preliminary analysis of knowledge, which overemphasises a certain view of the cognitive. I spent some time insisting upon a fairly generous interpretation of 'knowledge' – of the cognitive component in any mental activity – although such generosity is by no means idiosyncratic or prescriptive. It is very much in tune with how we generally use the word. Too narrow a definition of knowledge neglects the practical knowledge, the 'know-how', and instead concentrates upon propositional knowledge, the 'know that', and this is what Hirst tends to do. In consequence many activities that we engage in, and that I would seek to have upon the curriculum, give way to statements about those activities. Art becomes either aesthetic or itself a specific kind of statement; morality becomes moral judgement; literary criticism tends to supplant writing or enjoying literature. Important though it is to know *that* certain statements are true, knowing *how* to do things (to play a piece of music, to enjoy a concert, to make a sketch, to appreciate a poem, to climb skilfully) is equally a cognitive achievement, a development of the mind, which is not reducible to 'knowing that' or to the kinds of knowledge that can be stated in propositions. Hirst is preoccupied with propositional knowledge. So too is much of our curriculum. And that is a mistake, because it involves a mistaken philosophy of mind and it imposes too many academic restraints upon an otherwise educational programme.

My second disagreement with Hirst is in the reduction of knowledge (even propositional knowledge) into seven fundamental kinds. According to Hirst, 'a liberal education approached directly in terms of disciplines will thus be composed of the study of at least paradigm examples of all the various forms of knowledge'. But how is one to adjudicate what counts as paradigm examples of different forms of knowledge? This is not made clear. Presumably, paradigms will be those frameworks, structures or models of enquiry which manifest most explicitly the logical features which define a form of knowledge. For example, 'many sections of physics are probably more comprehensive and clear in logical character, more typical of the well developed physical sciences than, say, botany'. The assumption is therefore that

39

the logical features of a 'form' are decided independently of the choice of paradigms. How else would we know what a paradigm is a paradigm of?

However, the contrary could be argued – and must be argued in the absence (as in Hirst's argument) of any independent deduction of a limited number of fundamental forms – namely, that it is the choice of paradigm which determines how the form of knowledge is to be characterised. Thus the botanist might plausibly argue that to see his studies as a pale reflection of a form of knowledge *best* exemplified in physics is to misunderstand what he is doing; they are different activities defined in terms of different approaches to a specific set of problems, although sharing some general conceptual features. And indeed, in the absence of some independent (or a priori) argument for these forms of knowledge, characterised by these central concepts and these modes of verification, there is no logical reason against a proliferation of forms of knowledge, depending on the choice of paradigms.

The attempt to give a fundamental characterisation of these distinct forms is confused. According to Hirst and Peters (1970, p.64) a 'form' is identified by the 'fundamental, ultimate, or categoreal concepts of a most general kind which other concepts in the category presuppose'. They constitute 'the form' of thought, as opposed to its content. For example, 'space', 'time', and 'cause' are the categoreal concepts of the physical sciences which are presupposed by such concepts as 'acid', 'electron', or 'velocity'. A logical distinction, then, is drawn between concepts as categories (i.e. those which define a form of thought and 'inform' all other concepts) and concepts which are dispensable or which constitute the particular developments of that form of knowledge at a particular stage. This is a perfectly intelligible distinction, and it enters especially into the developmental and curriculum thinking of Piaget, but it runs into difficulties when put to Hirst's particular use. Hirst extends the notion of categoreal

40

concept from concepts that do seem fundamental, in the sense that it is inconceivable we could ever do without them (e.g. concepts of causal connection between material objects within a spatio-temporal framework), to a whole variety of concepts such as 'God' and 'ought' that do not seem fundamental in that same sense. There is a shift in the meaning of 'categoreal'.

Firstly there is a notion of category as a necessary condition, not of a particular form of thought, but of any thought whatsoever. Thus we logically must think within a conceptual framework of space and time. We are necessarily confined to ways of thinking that involve reference to material objects in space and in time. Secondly there is a notion of category as fundamental to a way of thinking (it picks out a central area of interest) where however that way of thinking is not indispensable. Thus 'God' might be a central concept of religious forms of thinking in a way that 'prayer' is not ('prayer' presupposes a concept of 'God', but not vice versa), but it is conceivable that someone would never think in religious terms. Hence, 'God' would not be a fundamental category of thought in the same sense that 'space' and 'time' are. Thirdly, Hirst includes amongst his categoreal concepts those that play an important, structuring part in a mode of thinking but which are dispensable even to that mode of thinking. 'Ought' is not a defining characteristic of moral discourse in the way that 'God' is of religious discourse. A system of morals is conceivable that appraised persons more than actions, and listed virtues rather than duties.

Since 'categoreal' concepts define a form of knowledge, this ambiguity enters into the very meaning of Hirst's 'forms'. Forms of knowledge are not, qua forms, defined in the same logical manner — or (put more crudely) Hirst pitches his 'central concepts' at too many different levels. The curriculum consequences of this criticism are important. If central concepts are to be understood as categoreal in the first sense (as a necessary condition), then the conse-

41

quent forms of knowledge are the indispensable modes of thought that determine the legitimate features of all thinking (even the unformulated, commonsense thinking of everyday chat of the primary school). If in the second sense (as fundamental to a way of thinking), however, the central concepts are not indispensable to thinking as such but only to the kind of thinking which they enter into as defining terms. But to work out what these are and what would count as a comprehensive account of them would be a different philosophical job from analysing the most fundamental categories of thought. If in the third sense (as dispensable though important) the central concepts do not enter into the definition of any distinctive and fundamental form of knowledge, or, if they do, there would be an immense proliferation of forms. Personally I am quite happy with such a proliferation of forms. My argument in this chapter is levelled against the kind of reductionist exercise performed by Phenix and Hirst. But, given such a proliferation, given the variety and extent of human achievement, the whole notion of fundamental forms becomes redundant.

Hirst, then, (as with Phenix) proposes, prior to curriculum planning, a limited and fundamental categorisation of cognition. In so doing, he rightly indicates the complex way in which we structure experience. But, in being more specific about the organisation of knowledge for curriculum purposes, either he does not do justice to the complex differences between disciplined enquiries into many different kinds of problems, or, in attempting to make sense of these differences, he provides an antecedent scheme of thought into which all these different ways of enquiring, thinking, arguing have to be made to fit. Such a scheme is not fully argued at the philosophical level; its articulation involves a confused notion of central organising or categoreal concepts, and it imposes an ill-fitting framework within which to examine critically the many activities competing for a place on the curriculum.

4. Literature and the fine arts as a form of knowledge

I wish to complete this chapter by examining briefly one suggested 'form of knowledge'. This will be a useful example of the general position outlined in the previous section. But my main purpose is not to extend my examination or criticism of that position further, but rather to indicate the much more complex view of human achievement that lies beneath the relationship I wish to establish between knowledge and schooling.

According to Hirst (1965) literature and the fine arts constitute one form of knowledge. Consequently whatever counts as a piece of literature and whatever claims to be a work of art would have certain features in common which distinguishes them from all other kinds of knowledge – religious, mathematical, and so on. On Hirst's argument this means that all literature and all works of fine art would be characterised by certain central organising concepts and distinctive tests of truth.

However, my immediate intuitive response to this is that such a philosophical view is in danger of making the many creative and artistic activities that we have come to value fit a very limiting and distorting framework which defines beforehand what is legitimately to count as literature or as art. The rich and varied achievement of mankind is in danger of being reduced (for curriculum purposes) to the essential characteristics of a particular predefined form, and, in being so reduced, not seen for what it really is. The difficulty again is that of a narrow conception of what knowledge is and thus of what it is for the mind to grow and to develop.

These difficulties can be best illustrated through Hirst's (1973) defence of 'literature and the fine arts as a unique form of knowledge', and through two criticisms of this. According to Hirst '. . . the physically observable features of shape, colour, sound, etc. have a significance that parallels the shape and sound of words and sentences we use in making statements about the physical world'. Hence in the

43

arts 'the observable features are used as symbols, have meaning, can be seen as making artistic statements and judged true or false just as words and sentences can be used to make scientific statements'. Furthermore, such artistic statements state 'truths that cannot be communicated in any other way'. The issue, then, as to literature and art being a unique form of knowledge, turns on whether works of literature and art can in all cases be appraised as true or false, for such is the condition for anything being a statement.

If they are to be seen as true or false statements, what makes them true cannot be some sort of correspondence with the real sensible world which they are somehow describing, for, as such, works of art would not be a unique form of knowledge, only a slightly bizarre way of giving an empirical account of the world. (Some works of art might be that as well.) At the same time, although such a simple form of correspondence between artefact and reality will not do, as *statements* works of art must be saying something about a reality that in some sense exists independently of the statements themselves or (as in mathematics) about a development, strictly according to well defined rules, of equations from explicitly formulated axioms. The independence of the external reality, or of the well defined rules of proceeding, gives the possibility of testing the truth or falsity of my statement. But it is not at all clear from Hirst's argument what this independent element is with which I can 'compare' or test out the artistic statements. And unless such an independent element can be given, then it is not clear to me how works of art can continue to be classed as statements or art itself as a unique form of knowledge.

Certain difficulties in this thesis are argued by Scrimshaw (1973). Firstly, there are certain general features of language – its conventional nature, its translatability, its construction through semantic and syntactical rules from basic units (words) – which are not shared by works of art. Secondly, to understand works of art as statements raises further problems. To be a statement the work of art is either true or false. False statements would be the negation of the true statements. We can conceive of the negation of such statements as 'Water boils at 100°'. But what conceivably could be the negation of the Mona Lisa?

These important analytic points, however, simply underline the main difficulty as pointed out by Reid (1974). The development of mind does indeed require an extension and refinement of knowledge, but knowledge is not necessarily – not even centrally – to be understood as propositional (knowledge that). '. . . The words of the poem . . . must be read with a feeling for the values, which feeling is finely embodied in the sound, rhythm, balance, direction and varying weight of the subtly constructed patterns of words.' Similarly with other works of art – these are creations for enjoyment rather than for making truth claims, although such enjoyment is intelligent, including 'all the different aspects of consciousness, cognitive, conative, affective, as enjoyed by the embodied person acutely aware'.

The point is that works of art are intelligently engaged in; they do require some conception of what one is doing and of the materials one is working with; they involve skills and know-how, and they involve standards of appraisal even if these be to some extent unique to the actual work of art. A poem might forge its own criteria of value, as well as conform to other criteria. But such intelligent involvement, giving pleasure or satisfaction, and requiring both conceptualising what one is doing and being disciplined by standards of successful performance, in no way entails a propositional kind of knowledge, a 'knowledge that' which must be either true or false.

Summary

1 The development of mind lies in the disciplined way in which one comes to engage in various activities, and this is

partly acquired through participation in socially developed ways of acting and thinking.

2 Such disciplined activities do provide structured subject-matters from which the teacher can draw curriculum content. Structure is provided by the concepts employed, the ways of proceeding, the criteria of achievement, and the problems tackled.

3 Phenix and Hirst have attempted to reduce these different subject-matters to a few general categories which provide the planning basis for systematic initiation into public modes of thought and experience. But such reductionism is unjustified.

4 Aesthetics is one example of this reductionism. But, instead of such a priori categorising of what people do, one should attend more carefully to the variety of disciplined activities they do in fact engage in.

Further reading
One of the best short introductions to the notion of mental disciplines is Schwab (1964). Other contributions of Ford and Pugno (1964) illustrate the meaning of 'structure' through particular disciplinary activities. Schwab (1969) develops his ideas further in the context of higher education. Hirst (1974) gathers together various extensions of his ideas about forms of knowledge, and part 2 of Phenix (1964) gives details of his realms of meaning for particular subject areas. Bruner (1960) gives an invaluable account of his notion of structure and its significance to curriculum development. A generous view of cognitive development related in particular to the arts, morality, religion, and personal knowledge with which I feel considerable sympathy is to be found in Reid (1961). In Units 11 and 12 of the Open University course E203, *Curriculum, Design and Development,* I have developed these ideas in a more practical context than this book aims at. See Pring (1976).

3 EDUCATING INTERESTS

1. The Child-centred philosophy

W. H. Kilpatrick spoke of the childrens' interests determining curricular content and structure, and of common learnings resulting from common interests. In introducing the account of *An Experiment with a Project Curriculum* (see Collings 1923) he denied that the aims of the school were 'conventional knowledge or skills'. The alternative starting-point was 'the actual present life of the boys and girls themselves, with all their interests and desires, good and bad'; the first step was 'to help guide these children to choose the most interesting and fruitful parts of this life as the content of their school activity'; and the consequent aims were

> first to help the boys and girls do better than they otherwise would the precise things they had chosen, and second, by means of the experience of choosing and through the experience of the more effectual activity gradually to broaden the outlook of the boys and girls as to what they might further choose and then help them better effect these new choices.

The curriculum then would not be the subjects or subject-matters chosen by the teacher, which the pupil would be persuaded to learn or to master, but would focus rather upon

47

what was already effectively engaging the mind of the child. Anything else could not be educative for (although in some sense it might be learnt or memorised) it would, as it were, be superficially stuck on. It would not help change or transform the thoughts, feelings, desires, wishes and aspirations which make up the life of the mind.

Kilpatrick represents an important tradition in curriculum thinking that is rarely treated by philosophers of education with the seriousness which for several reasons it deserves. Firstly, there is much popular talk about basing the curriculum upon the interests of the pupils, about bridging the gulf between what is prescribed on the curriculum for the pupils and what in practice the pupils are interested in. Secondly, there are good ethical reasons why this should be so. Finally, the alternative view – the prescription of a particular curriculum content or subject-matter initially alien to the pupils' questions, puzzles and mode of thinking – puts into focus my starting question: why should *this* ('foreign' subject-matter that it is) be educative for *these* (whose minds are engaged in quite different pursuits)?

Despite popular talk about basing the curriculum upon the interests of the pupil, this rarely happens in practice. Certainly teachers seek to make their material interesting or seek to harness what they, the teachers, want to teach onto some current interest of the pupil. For example, various aspects of mathematics are learnt through measurement of the school's football pitch or by working out Division I goal averages, both of which are supposed to be interests of, say, eleven-year-olds. But this is not focusing the curriculum upon the interests of the pupils (i.e. what their minds are persistently and thoughtfully engaged with and what therefore needs to be educated). On this view, simply to harness what the teacher wants to teach onto the pupils' current interest is to *dis*respect what the pupils really find valuable and thus to *dis*count the pupils' most influential and formative thoughts. It is to trivialise these. To *use* interests in this way is basically to leave the central core of the child's mental life where it is. It is not then to educate *him*.

On the other hand to try to make the material more interesting is, on this view, to trivialise the material. It is to say that the subject-matter offered has nothing to say to the pupil despite the fact that he has a mind already actively engaged in a wide range of thoughtful activities. It is informally to acknowledge the disconnection between knowledge as something exterior to the knowing subject and knowing as a process by which man (and this pupil in particular) organises experience more or less effectively for a variety of purposes.

The plausibility of this position gains credence from the need to make educational sense of one's belief that *all* are candidates for educational salvation, despite the rejection by large numbers of pupils of the so-called educative subject-matter presented by the school. What is it to educate these pupils? Well, look at them and see. Observe what is really engaging their attention, what really matters to them, and then assist them to develop the relevant capacities, to value more satisfactorily, to perceive more accurately, to develop whatever qualities of mind are already at work or will be required in those activities that have already 'caught on'. The young child is curious about worms – where they live, how they eat, why they wriggle. Such curiosity can be neglected, allowed to die through unanswered questions. Or it can be seized upon and met through explanations that require close (and assisted) observation and new ideas for organising the child's way of thinking. Such new facts, or new organisation of thought, will only be an intermediate stage in the mental development of the child; they will both present and stimulate yet further puzzles and questions, which in turn will require new observations, new reformulation of the ever changing conceptual schemes of the young child. The adolescent too will have his puzzles and questions, his doubts and his absorbing interests. Through these, or through meeting these, new concepts will be introduced, old

49

ones sharpened or transformed, facts made available, paths of enquiry suggested. In this way he will develop a more adequate set of thoughts to meet his particular purposes. But these will not be self-contained. The development of thought in one area will affect thinking in another, raising yet further questions or doubts where once there was certainty. The mind, on this view, is an actively questioning, doubting, puzzling, adapting, organising 'organism' that cannot in practice be divided into separate parts, even if the theorist (as a result of logical analysis) might do so for his own purposes.

The immediate objection to this view of curriculum and to this way in which the mind is to be assisted in its development is that there is something so piecemeal, so arbitrary about such an education. The mind will be expanded, enlightened and extended only so far as the current interests and curiosities of the child will permit. And these are provincial indeed. The tension here then is between those on the one hand who believe that there are a limited number of fairly well delineated subject-matters which the pupil is initially on the outside of and into which he needs to be initiated, and those on the other who see no difference in kind, no significant or logical gap, between the thinking of the young child and that of the expert – the one leads on to the other if properly guided. I find myself caught up within this tension. Why?

Firstly, I wish to hold on to my initial statement that education must ultimately be about the development of John's mind or Mary's thoughts, and these are already present, formed and operating in a very active way. And this view is confirmed by my experience as pupil, student, and teacher, which has demonstrated vividly how so much of school and university knowledge leaves the learner as he is. It provides occasions maybe for displays of cleverness but in no way is the pupil or student affected or transformed by the experience. The mind has not been opened up to new possibilities, to new values or ways of looking at things. School trippers to the Austrian Alps rest content only when their favourite pop star has been discovered on the local record machine. The imagination remains unaffected by what the school has provided.

Secondly, however, my argument in the last chapter, which insisted upon the public nature of the knowledge through which each individual's activity – his thoughts, desires, hopes, and tryings – is made more adequate. The mind of each one of us participates in a world of meanings and of values that has been socially developed. Furthermore such developments are achievements, worthy of our respect and emulation. They extend the powers of the mind more effectively than hitherto; they successfully tackle problems that hitherto had been a stumbling block, or they feed the imagination, open up yet further lines of fruitful enquiry, engage the mind in a more satisfactory and pleasurable way. The teacher must see his role as the mediator of such cultural achievements and from such well defined subject-matter, which represents the infinite variety of the achievements of mankind, the teacher must draw in order to help develop the life of the mind of each pupil.

Hence, in brief, the 'child-centred' view, represented at the beginning of this chapter by Kilpatrick, focuses our attention upon the already active minds of individual children, minds which have already been developed in their manifold activity long before they reach a teacher and which must be the ultimate reference point of any educational activity or programme. It says 'don't forget that the child is a living thing, with thoughts and beliefs, hopes and choices, feelings and wishes; helping him with these must be what education is about, for there is nothing else to educate'. On the other hand there can be detected in such a view a too easy dismissal of the ways of thinking, believing, hoping, choosing, feeling and wishing, developed and made available by others, which may not have immediate relevance to the

51

current preoccupations of the pupil. This, I think, is what people find objectionable in the 'child-centred' view represented by Kilpatrick. What then are the arguments for such a dismissal? They seem to be basically of two kinds, one is an ethical argument, the other about the nature of knowledge.

2. The ethical argument

What gives the child-centred philosophers of education (I am thinking particularly of Dewey and Kilpatrick and latterly P. S. Wilson) force and significance is the underlying theory of value reflected in their concern for the 'interests' of the child. A distinction is made between what is judged by society to be useful for the child and what the child intrinsically values for its own sake. It may be necessary for a society to train technicians and thus for the school or college to help with this task of training. It will teach those skills, that know-how which is deemed by society to be of value, but at the same time the persons trained may remain, in a very real sense, hardly affected. They have acquired some extra techniques and skills certainly, they have had, as it were, something stuck on to them, but this something has not really become part of them and will just as easily come unstuck. Their imagination and aspirations, their questionings and puzzles, their values and concerns remain more or less where they were before.

Does this sound so very strange? Anyone engaged in training students for 'O' levels or even degrees must have seen this countless times – a 'learning off' or a 'sticking on' of subject-matter that somehow leaves the person where he was before. The child-centred philosophers would want to say that such experiences are not educative; they in no way, or hardly at all, transform the person, the subject of the exercise, whose personality lies in an already rich and varied set of thoughtful activities. These, the real objects of an educational programme, are left where they were.

The ethical argument goes further. What is judged valuable by society may not then be valued by the recipient (he remains largely unaffected and indifferent – or indeed bored and alienated): it will have no intrinsic value for him. Its value then must be in what it does for society or for the individual later (e.g. a better job or more money). What is done therefore would be done not for its intrinsic worth (because on the whole the pupils find no worth in it) but because it is, extrinsically speaking, valuable in acquiring some other 'good'. Ultimately however (so the argument goes) we must arrive at some goods that are intrinsically worthwhile – which require no further justification in terms of what other goods they will produce. Otherwise we have an infinite regress. But, say the child-centred philosophers, what are these intrinsically worthwhile things other than what people find worthwhile, want to possess or engage in, find satisfying and pleasurable, freely make the object of their choice? Whatever is judged valuable must ultimately be so judged because of what is intrinsically valuable and no basis can be found for what is intrinsically valuable other than that people value it or choose it willingly and freely, e.g. take an interest in it.

Wilson (1971, p.67) makes this point in the following way:

> a child's education [as opposed to schooling] can only proceed through the pursuit of his interests since it is only these which are of intrinsic value . . . [and] whatever enables him to appreciate and understand his interests more fully and to pursue them more actively and effectively is educative.

Remember the argument is essentially an ethical one. How do we justify making children attend school, even when they do not want to go or attach no value to it? The justification criticised by the child-centred philosophers lies in a theory of value which says that certain activities and experiences are (objectively speaking) so worthwhile that we feel free to impose them upon unwilling pupils who do not appreciate their worth. Value or worthwhileness therefore would, on this view, be defensible even when people in fact do not (subjectively) value what is judged by others to be of value. Some activities or experiences would be, in some objective sense, more worthwhile than others (e.g. a piece of classical music more than pop) even though they were not in fact valued or seen to be worthwhile. But, say the child-centred philosophers, what is the basis of such an ethical view? How do you justify one kind of activity or experience to be more worthwhile than another independently of whether or not the recipients do find value in it? Basic, then, to the child-centred view is a deep seated suspicion of an educational programme that presupposes some objective hierarchy of values in which, say, classical music is better than pop, pure science superior to applied, Lewis Carroll more worthwhile than Enid Blyton, even though the majority of pupils might think otherwise (and show their thinking through yawns and distracted behaviour).

In many ways the ethical difficulty is like that posed by the Utilitarians. Must not the value of anything lie ultimately in the pleasure and satisfaction which it gives? The Utilitarians (in particular Jeremy Bentham, James Mill and John Stuart Mill) could find no other defence of what was judged to be worthwhile than that it brought more pleasure and satisfaction than otherwise.

Of course, it would be wrong to construe 'pleasure' in a purely hedonistic sense, and there are many parallels between Mill's (1863, chapter 2) defence of utilitarianism against his critics and Wilson's (1971 and 1967) defence of a child-centred view of education against his (especially Peters 1967). For example, Mill was at pains to point out that what people find pleasurable are not only sensual (such seemed to be the connotation in a puritan age) but intellectual activities

– in whatever people found satisfaction and maintained their interest. Similarly Wilson constantly argues that it is wrong to say (as many critics have) that what is based upon the interests of the child would necessarily be trivial. For the child already has thoughts and feelings which are very significant for *him*; he is already the subject of influences that are transforming *him*; he is already engaged in thoughtful activities which will change *his* environment and the way *he* will live. And such interests (which hold his attention) are trivial neither in the sense of the importance he attaches to them nor in the sense of what they do to him.

But the objections to the child-centred ethics are not vanquished quite so easily. Belief in the superiority of certain activities and experiences over others is too deep within our way of thinking to be dismissed lightly. Has it not infiltrated into every aspect of our social life – whether in our readiness to accept government subsidies for certain activities but not for others, or in the choice of certain resources (certain stimulating environments) rather than others for our children? As a father, I encourage certain reading rather than others, expose my children to certain environmental experiences rather than others, encourage certain activities rather than others, because I believe that they are in some sense better or more worthwhile, however difficult I find it to justify this.

Yet at the same time, despite my inability to reject completely some objective hierarchy of values (and I have never seen anyone in practice reject it, only in theory) there is a very real sense in which the child must come to see their value if they are to be valuable to him. Furthermore the value of what is offered must partly lie in the possibility it provides for giving satisfaction and pleasure, for sustaining interest, for being found to be valuable by the child. And there is a sense therefore in which the child is not being educated by my music or my Latin teaching if he does not come to see the value in it, if he remains bored and alienated, possibly even

55

less capable of finding it valuable after my attempts.

Whatever reservations one may feel about an unqualified child-centred view, Dewey and Kilpatrick were surely right in insisting that the educative value of an experience was partly in the pupils finding value and interest in it. Consequently they were surely right in identifying miseducation with whatever activities and experiences bored children, turned them off, made them disvalue what was on offer. I want my children to learn how to play an instrument, to appreciate music, because of the pleasure, the satisfaction, the mind absorbing interests, the transforming quality that such activities in general have. But at the same time I can only offer these possibilities. Unless they come to see these values, far from educating, their music lessons could so easily be miseducative, no matter how clever they become in answering quizzes about music or in getting certificates of proficiency.

3. The cognitive argument

Just as the ethical argument says that the value of what is offered by the school is proportionate to the value that the pupil finds in it, so the cognitive argument says that the meaning (and thus the truth) of what is offered is proportionate to its meaningfulness for each pupil (and to its 'working' for him). Furthermore just as the critics of the child-centred theory of value wish to maintain the worthwhileness of the curriculum independently of whether the child finds worth in it, so the critics of the child-centred theory of knowledge wish to maintain a more objective status for the knowledge and meaning which are on offer. Knowledge does, in the critics' view, somehow exist independently of individual knowers.

The argument begins from the premiss that a given set of beliefs, a particular state of knowledge (if you like, a particular subject-matter), is ultimately rooted in some original attempt to solve problems. The meaning of any kind of knowledge or of any particular subject-matter cannot be disconnected either from the problems or from the attempts to meet those problems. Knowledge, then, and the subject-matters that are offered through the curriculum are a particular stage in the active attempt to find a solution to a problem. And the solution is provisional – it remains a solution so long as the original puzzle is satisfied, so long, that is, as it continues to work for the enquirer. In being meaningful, it is meaningful to this or that person who shares the problem for which it is offered as a solution; it is not meaningful in itself.

Hence it would be mistaken for the teacher to present the product of enquiry (others' enquiries) as though it were meaningful in itself, as though it were true or false independently of either the problems for which it is a provisional settlement or the processes by which it has been reached. Knowledge is not independent of the problems that puzzle particular people or of the proceses ds which they meet those problems; the 'truth' of what is arrived at (and then transmitted) is not independent of the satisfaction given to the original enquirer. There has always been a pragmatic theory of meaning and truth underlying the child-centred philosophy, and this is reflected in the current popular conflation of 'meaning' with 'relevance', of 'truth' with 'effectiveness', of 'knowledge' with 'satisfactory settlement of enquiry'.

Maybe the more popular manifestation and spirit of such pragmatism is captured by Goldsmiths College Curriculum Laboratory (1969, p.6) when it says:

enquiry pulls us away from thinking of education as a diet composed of subjects, back to a more central concern with enabling young people to interfere with and to respond to the world, to live out their instinctual demands, maintaining the drive of curiosity in thinking for themselves.

Education is not (it is claimed) a matter of introducing pupils to a body of truths which are the same for everybody. The 'truthful perceptions' that 'emerge' relate to the particular enquiries, questions and understandings of each child. The organisation of the curriculum therefore would be based on those particular enquiries, questions and understandings, rather than on the end products of others' enquiries (doubtless in response to other questions) reflected in different branches of learning. According to James (1968), then director of the curriculum laboratory, the teacher's task is not 'to induct pupils into known certainties' but to 'invite them to collaborate into explorations of the unknown . . . new possibilities of moral order, new developments in knowledge, new kinds of internal social relationships and new relationships with the larger community'. As a consequence of learning necessarily arising out of the interested enquiry of the pupil, the 'role of the teacher' changes from that of an instructor, giving a class lesson, to that of a 'facilitator, an impressario, and a consultant'. The teaching role changes, according to James, because knowledge is no longer 'a central objective of the curriculum'; there is no such thing as stable knowledge to be taught; enquiry rather than knowledge becomes the focal point of organisation, and the goal of education is 'the facilitation of change and learning' or 'learning how to learn'.

So much for a particular, popular manifestation of child-centredness. What however are its philosophical roots, or at least its roots in a theory of knowledge?

Dewey (1933) gives an account of how we think – how the child or the adult, in pursuing some interest or enquiry, goes through different phases of reflective thinking. The limits of every 'unit' of thinking (whether it be the professor puzzling over a complex problem in mathematics or the child reflecting upon the refusal of the fish to bite his maggots) are, at the beginning, 'a perplexed, troubled, or confused situation' and, at the end, a 'cleared-up, unified, resolved situa-

58

tion', resulting in a 'direct experience of mastery, satisfaction, enjoyment'. From (i), the state of perplexity, arises (ii), suggestions of solution, and (iii), an 'intellectualisation' of the perplexity felt into a problem to be solved. Such intellectualisations are followed by (iv), ideas or hypotheses to guide efforts to resolve the perplexity, and (v), elaboration of the ideas or hypotheses (a kind of reasoning out the consequences of holding this hypothesis). Finally there is (vi), the testing out of the hypothesis by overt or imaginative action, before (vii), satisfaction or resolution of the perplexity.

Elsewhere Dewey (1916 and 1938 particularly) argues for the relevance of this theory to the curriculum. In general he concludes that

(i)   The logical ordering of subject-matter into different kinds is rooted in enquiry.
(ii) The process of enquiry itself is roughly of the same kind in its different manifestations.
(iii) This unitary process rather than the differentiated product should be the focal point of the curriculum.
(iv) The differentiated product (the different subject-matters) should no more than help the teacher in directing the pupil along the most fruitful lines of his enquiry.

One practical consequence of such a theory of enquiry, especially under the influence of Kilpatrick (1918), was the popularity of 'the project method'. Its influence lay not only in stimulating other people to write other books but also in classroom practice in Britain as well as in America. The insistence upon projects in primary as well as in the lower forms of some secondary schools would find a philosophical defence in the cognitive theory of Dewey and Kilpatrick (whether or not its practical exponents would recognise or have recourse to it).

59

But note how quickly schools assume the child-centred ethos of such a philosophical position without its substance. Projects abound but they are so often the teachers' projects not the childrens'; they begin with the teachers' perplexity (or the teachers' conception of what the pupils ought to be perplexed about) not with what really perplexes the children. How rarely does one find child-centred education in the sense outlined by Kilpatrick and Dewey. So much for the rhetoric of the so-called child-centred educationalists of today! What they do and what they say they do rarely connect. (But I have seen schools where they do connect.)

There are difficulties, however, in holding such a view. Let us return to the popular expression of it again before a more philosophical examination is embarked upon. According to the Goldsmiths College Curriculum Laboratory (1969, p.14)

each problem will be different, giving rise to different questions, none of which can be anticipated by or fitted into preconceived categories. As a result of his experience, a child will want to ask questions; since no two people have the same response to any given experience, the questions each individual will want to ask . . . will also differ; *it is impossible for anyone else to know precisely what the child already understands* and what is the next question to which he needs the answer. (italics mine)

A more enquiry and project based curriculum (so long as it is the child's enquiry or project, resulting from the child's perplexity) provides the opportunity 'to redefine the relationships between process and knowledge', the process being one of 'reconstructing reality' through 'negotiation' with other constructs, and the knowledge being what is an adequate reconstruction for an individual's particular purposes (an 'interpretation that works').

On such a view, however, the teacher's words must mean something different to each pupil, for each has thoughts

60

arising from different perplexities and each therefore inhabits differently constructed realities. Only recently have I realised how much this way of thinking has entered into educational talk; it is now a commonplace in seminars to talk of the multiple realities of the classroom or each child having a differently structured set of experiences. But how far can one go before one has to admit solipsism? Possibly that situation is never reached in practice because a solipsist will have no one left to admit his solipsism to. No wonder there are so many anxious brows around institutes of education.

The seeds of such pragmatism are already sowed, you might say, in my opening chapters where I argue that a concept is a principle of unity in one's experience and that each growing child is constructing a conceptual scheme that is more or less adequate for his purposes. The need for communication will require the constant testing out of such a scheme upon others – like a testing out of hypotheses – and it will be found more or less adequate, more or less in need of constant redefinition, elaboration, and refinement. Moreover, I argued that the very complex conceptual systems of the adult were constantly being adapted and changed as they were found to be unable to cope with new situations and discoveries. The history of thought, as I said, is a history of conceptual change. And the reformulations of the specialists eventually percolate down to the language of everyday usage.

It would be wrong, however, from the developing nature both of a community's way of looking at the world and of an individual's gradual attainment of that way, to argue that each is constructing a reality unique to him, that 'it is impossible for anyone else to know precisely what the child already understands', that anyone's construction of reality is as good or as adequate as anyone else's, or that what is true (what counts as knowledge) is simply what works for that person. Remember that I have talked about two kinds of conceptual development. There is the formation of concepts by a group

61

of people over a period of time, the gradual development of a public set of meanings given permanence in language and thus made accessible. And there is the gradual attainment by individuals of such public meanings. In teaching we are clearly concerned primarily with the second kind of development – the introduction of our pupils to those different meanings, made accessible through language and through different traditions of thought and action, that mankind has achieved and that are adequate for a wide range of purposes. Such adequacy is not an arbitrary matter, nor does it result in pragmatism. As I took pains to explain in the second chapter, what is adequate or not as a description, explanation, or prescription, depends partly on what is the case (independently of one's feeling satisfied or not) and that is not a pragmatic matter. This rather important point will be developed further in the next chapter.

My criticism therefore of the cognitive theory of the child-centred philosophy is threefold. Firstly, there is a theory of meaning which stresses individual adjustment and individual construction of reality at the expense of public meanings made accessible through language and traditions of thought. Secondly, the product of enquiry becomes less significant than the process, the truth or falsity of what is said less important than the satisfaction achieved in getting there. Finally, the unity of enquiry is stressed to the neglect of the differences between kinds of enquiry, to the neglect of the wide range of different kinds of activity to which pupils might be introduced. Dewey and Kilpatrick were, in my view, yet further examples of those who sought greater unity in the universe than the universe permits.

4. Where do we go from here?
Despite these criticisms these philosophers were stressing important truths which are so often neglected. There is an important connection between the product of enquiry and

the process, between the conclusion of a thoughtful activity and the trials and difficulties of arriving there, between the conceptual framework through which one looks at the world and the sort of problems and puzzles which find a solution in these concepts. To teach historical fact, the product of historical enquiry, without exposing to view either the perplexities which gave rise to historical enquiry or the processes of selection and sifting and asking and criticism through which such perplexities were resolved, does a disservice to a way of thought, to a disciplined mode of enquiry. Indeed, the meaning of what is learnt would be partly lost. That William the Conqueror came to England in 1066 is true or false, and can be learnt as such independently of my being aware of the historical enquiry which has reached and made available this conclusion. But its historical significance (as with the historical insignificance of his sneezing in the same year) can only be grasped from an entry into the perplexities and puzzles of historical thinking. The recognition of this has indeed stimulated quite a lot of curriculum change. Projects in history (e.g. the Schools Council History 13-16) and science (e.g. the Schools Council Science 5-13) have stressed the importance of enquiry, of the children engaging with historical and scientific problems that give point to enquiry. But is this generally true? Does not even the teaching of Nuffield science so frequently return to the learning of conclusions? The content has changed but the process, the teaching process, that is, often remains the same. The educative value of introducing children to different traditions of thought and enquiry must lie partly in the resulting imaginative grasp of the kind of worries and anxieties that provoked both the development of traditions of enquiry and individual contributions to these traditions from which we all might draw and benefit. Why is the history of science, especially the biography of scientists, neglected on science curricula – one way surely of gaining imaginatively an understanding of what science is and has been about?

63

In my criticism of that school of educational philosophy which stresses the individual adjustment to environment – the individual reconstruction of his reality in so adjusting, the individual meaningfulness of what is offered in terms of his problems and his questionings – I have insisted upon the public nature of the meanings and achievements which it is the teacher's job to make accessible to his students or pupils. At the same time I have stressed that it is the individual's mind already active, already engaged in a multitude of thoughts and questionings, which is to be educated. Not only is it *there* that one must start, it is also *that* which needs to be respected. The teacher, from within more refined, more adequate, more developed traditions of thought and meaning, is indeed a resource to help those pupils find a more refined, adequate, and developed mode of doing what they are already doing. The tension therefore lies in having both a respect for each individual's way of thinking, feeling, and questioning, while retaining a belief in the superiority of the more public traditions of thought that, as a teacher, one represents and can introduce to the pupils. Unless one has a belief in the superiority of one's own way of thinking and the relevance of this to the already active life of the child or student, one ought not to be teaching.

This tension I frequently feel strongly in seminars on diploma and M.A. courses. The group will contain widely experienced and intelligent teachers, each holding well formed views, based upon years of experience and reflection. On significant educational issues there will be differences within the group – reflecting differences in value, in belief, in the perspective from which questions are viewed, and in the way of conceptualising the problems. As seminar leader I must have a general view as to where we should be going, or at least a standpoint that has itself withstood critical appraisal and that can be the basis from which critical examination of others must be offered. At the same time such a standpoint must be brought into contact with the values and beliefs of each member of the group. Over a long period of time thoughtful engagement with a problem will be gradually transformed through this contact. Of course it is a mutual process. The teacher learns in teaching – in trying to make sense of another's point of view, in trying to articulate his or her own, in meeting objections, in trying to uncross the wires of communication. Despite this recognition of fallability the respect for others' points of view does not entail equality in a process of negotiating meanings. This then is the difficulty I find in teaching in higher education, and I do not think in principle it is very different at any stage of education: how can one both respect the thoughtful concerns of one's students, making them the focus of one's teaching, whilst at the same time preserving the superiority of one's own well tested standpoint which is to illuminate those various concerns? There is no straight answer to this; preserving the balance in one's teaching is an art to be acquired.

The balance is between the two extremes that colleges and universities are so prone to. On the one hand there are those who preserve the superiority of their standpoint by insulating it from criticism of their students, who are open to no reciprocal relationship with those who learn, and who therefore do not respect (do not accept as the reference point of their 'teaching' activity) the minds of the students. (I have long since come to doubt the educational value of most lecturing.) On the other hand there are those who are so anxious to respect the minds of those who come to learn, so ready to be open and to negotiate everything, that everything is equally valid, no standpoint superior to another, no set of beliefs more adequate than another, no position that the teacher will stake his professional reputation on. University then simply provides the framework in which equals can be brought together for mutual enlightenment. But the curriculum must lie between these extremes, focused on the actual thinking of the student but drawing upon public traditions of thought made accessible by the teacher.

Finally it should be noted that those who stress the open-ended project method, the focus upon the pupils' interests, the unified process of enquiry, may really be stressing the development of certain qualities of mind which, at some stages of schooling, are more important than specific skills or subject matter. This I touched on briefly in chapter 1, and shall do so again in chapter 7.

Summary
1 The child-centred tradition has similarly objected to the divorce of school learning from the mental preoccupations of individual learners. 2,3 The philosophical bases of this position are ethical (x is valuable for Tom if Tom values x) and epistemological (x is meaningful or x counts as knowledge if it is meaningful for Tom or if it works for him). There are difficulties in both positions, denying as they do objectivity in both ethics and the theory of knowledge. 4 But they stress an often neglected truth, viz. that for x to be valuable for anyone its value must be accessible to him and that public traditions of thought must connect with the actual thinking of particular people.

Further reading
There is no alternative to reading Dewey (1938) for a brief introduction to his educational ideas, (1916) for a lengthy exposition. Wilson (1971) is the best recent philosophical account of this tradition. A useful criticism is Archambault (1956).

4 NEW DEFINITIONS OF KNOWLEDGE

1. 'New directions' in sociology

Gorbutt and others (1972), writing about the 'new sociology of education', point to the 'emergence of an alternative paradigm'. This paradigm 'has important implications for the professional awareness of those engaged in education at all levels in that it challenges rather than reinforces prevailing practices and their underlying assumptions'. Such prevailing practices include treating knowledge as a commodity which is transmitted (or sold) to rather passive (and frequently unwilling) pupils; one underlying assumption of such practices is that knowledge is something out there, independent of people knowing. These practices and their underlying assumptions are then to be challenged by the 'emergent paradigm'.

This emergent paradigm, according to Gorbutt and others, postulates that society is 'socially constructed, sustained and changed through the ongoing interaction of men'. People, including pupils, are (within this paradigm) considered to be essentially active in contributing to the reconstruction, maintenance and change of the social reality in which they live and which gives meaning and significance to what they do. 'Man constantly makes his world in that he is continually faced with the problem of constructing his social reality, of making sense of the world'.

67

From the perspective of this paradigm different assumptions about knowledge are made: 'knowledge at all levels . . . becomes thoroughly relativised and the possibility of absolute knowledge is denied' (ibid.). Radically different approaches to classroom practice follow, assisting the pupils in reconstructing their realities through a 'negotiation' of meanings.

Knowledge, then, is 'redefined' because previous definitions (i.e. previous boundaries between kinds of knowledge as well as standards of truth and validity within kinds of knowledge) are now seen for what they are – social constructions legitimated by those in positions of power and control. Curricular knowledge is what is defined as knowledge by the school or university and institutionalised in subject departments and the examinations system. As such it has a history and is explicable in sociological terms. The new sociology, therefore, in treating as problematic the definitions and categories of knowledge that usually go unquestioned by those who teach or transmit it, is challenging the organisation of knowledge upon the curriculum, the unquestioning nature with which it is so frequently served up and learnt, and the status which is attributed to success within such questionable activities. It is saying that there are alternative ways of organising experience, of seeing how things are, and these, being equally valid, ought to be made equally available. Indeed the pupil's own viewpoint, his own construction of reality, needs to be respected, even though it does not fit those viewpoints, those categories 'legitimated' by the school.

There are many aspects of this new direction in sociological theorising which are stimulating and valuable – especially its criticism of previous sociological work in education. Firstly, to understand a social event (e.g. a school assembly) it is necessary to see it from the point of view of the participants – the perspectives that they bring to bear upon what is happening. To understand what is going on in a classroom it

68

is not enough simply to observe – to treat what is seen as a 'thing' that can (or could conceivably) be explained by laws of science (even social science), or that can be measured or treated statistically. Rather it is necessary to grasp the views, concepts and values that the participants bring to bear upon the situation. What is the case in a social situation is, at least in part, dependent upon the categories through which events are interpreted. For example, the teacher shouts at a pupil, but what exactly has happened depends upon the intention with which the sound is uttered. What may appear simply to the eye or to the ear to be the same thing may be interpreted quite differently if those shouts are seen to issue from different intentions, different conceptions of the situation.

Secondly, this new perspective in sociology challenges that kind of classroom practice which treats knowledge as a product, quite disconnected from the processes which have produced it. It quite rightly criticises the treatment of knowledge as a commodity to be handed on as such to rather passive learners. Genuine knowledge is not like that – it is a way of looking at the world, a perspective within which one sees things, acts, makes choices. What counts as knowledge must in some way transform the way in which one experiences the world.

Thirdly, this new direction in sociology points out the possibility of alternative ways of seeing things and of change within already established ways. The learner has a way of looking at and valuing things which may be different from that of the adult and which needs to be respected. The teacher, and even the authoritative bases of school knowledge, are not infallible. At no stage can one say 'this is it; no further development, correction, or change in a way of thinking is possible'. If any other impression is given at school, if the impression is given that what is taught is 'absolute' in the sense that it is immune from critical appraisal and from further development, then the sociologists are pointing a critical finger in the right direction.

69

Finally, the sociologists are pointing to the social context in which knowledge is developed and made available. I have constantly argued in this book that concepts through which we think, have a picture of the world, value things, make choices, are formed by communities of people. Specialist languages are forged by specialist groups, assisted by the formation of societies, are made accessible through journals and promoted through teaching institutions. There are detectable differences between the ways in which different communities conceptualise different aspects of reality. Some communities have greater discriminatory powers within their language than others do, just as the refinements of the English language have often been made more available to some speakers of that language than to others. Ways of thinking are socially constructed, and any philosophical accounts of curriculum knowledge must take into account both the social and the changing nature of how we think.

Despite these areas of agreement, and despite the welcome I readily extend to anyone who questions the reification of social reality (e.g. treating disciplined ways of thinking as 'disciplines') or who criticises the disconnection of product from the mode of production or who insists upon respect for the alternative ways of looking at things introduced to school by the pupil, the more extravagent claims that accompany such excellent points seem to me simply mistaken. There is a sense in which knowledge is independent of individual knowers and there are limits to the degree to which individuals can seek to 'redefine knowledge' or to 'reconstruct reality' or to 'negotiate meanings'. What that sense is and what those limits are I shall now attempt to show. I wish to maintain (despite my belief in the 'social construction of reality') the 'prevailing tradition within the philosophy of education', attacked by Maxine Greene and thereafter by her sociological followers (see Whitty 1974) which presents 'disciplines' or 'public traditions' or 'accumulated wisdom' or 'common culture' as 'objectively existent, external to the knower – there to be discovered, mastered, learnt'. But, of course, my defence of such a tradition has to be seen within the qualifications and elaborations that I have made in the preceding chapters where I have been almost repetitive in 'de-reifying' subjects and insisting upon the social context of knowledge.

2. Socially related and socially relative

A characteristic of disciplined activity implicit within its rule governed nature which I stressed earlier is that it is publicly accessible, open to public scrutiny and mastery. The procedures for finding out, for organising experiences, even for verifying the results of enquiry, are the refinements of many generations of social activity and are open to yet further refinements by those who have already mastered them.

Herein lies a philosophical point about the nature of knowledge which, if misunderstood, leads to relativism. The relativist position is as follows: since what counts as knowledge is a social product, and as such requires acceptance by those in the position to decide (the authorities), different forms of social life and different authorities produce different 'definitions of knowledge'. What counts as knowledge is relative to different social contexts. To understand, therefore, the development and differentiation of knowledge requires, not a philosophical analysis of knowledge claims but a sociological analysis of the forms of life which cause them and of the authorities who decide what is to count.

What follows for the curriculum? If the division and organisation of knowledge simply reflect the existing legitimising authorities, then to change the authorities would lead to a change in the definition of knowledge. Indeed, if on the other hand one attempted (subversively) to make a direct onslaught on the current definitions of knowledge, the authorities might disappear by default – there would be little purpose in appointing professors of geography if geography

71

was no longer recognised as a distinct area of intellectual activity. In either case, this recognition of the 'relative validity' of the current 'definitions of knowledge' would suggest a type of curriculum organisation in which knowledge divisions are not so tightly controlled – what Bernstein (1971) calls the 'weak classification' of an 'integrated code'.

In meeting these difficulties I in no way wish to withdraw my characterisations of a disciplined mode of enquiry as essentially a social activity, a social construct if you like, open to social criticism, adaptation, or development. In teaching a pupil a particular subject-matter – a particular kind of musical activity, biology, electronics – we are introducing him to a social enterprise, to a set of interests shared and contributed to by many others. He is entering into a tradition of identifying and tackling problems, and possibly the best way of entering into such a tradition is to be 'apprenticed' to a recognised practitioner. It has long since been recognised that teaching and research go together in higher education; rarely is the importance of this recognised in schools.

Furthermore, there are different intellectual disciplines (and different intellectual authorities) in so far as there are different socially acknowledged ways by which problems are identified, experience described, conclusions criticised, arguments evaluated. It is by becoming acquainted with the rules of a social activity (for example, by submitting to the criticism of others) that one internalises the capacity for disciplined thinking and thus for self-criticism.

This public and social character of disciplined activities is reflected, as I said, in the institutionalised way in which disciplines are protected and promoted – institutes, societies, journals, etc which emphasise the corporate nature of the activities they are engaged in. And this is, and must be, as much the case at school as at university level. School teachers of English and history have established their own societies and journals, subjects are given departmental structure within schools and, through these, certain implicit rules of arguing, evaluating, etc, come to be shared, developed and promoted. Yet despite this obvious dependence of knowledge and its promotion upon such institutional factors I wish to deny that such a sociological picture is the full story.

It might appear so, as clearly it does to some of the more radical critics of the differentiated curriculum. Thus from the philosophical truth that all knowledge is 'socially situated' and from the observation that the growth or stagnation of knowledge at particular periods (and its availability to particular people) can be contingently related to particular forms of social control, it is argued that all knowledge is socially determined, all truth is relative to particular 'legitimating' agencies. Ultimately the adoption of any theoretical framework (frequently referred to as a total ideology or a total paradigm) is an arbitrary choice. Recently, at a college of education, the B.Ed. students withdrew from the seminar of one lecturer in philosophy of education because they did not share her 'paradigm'. The validity of what was said had been legitimated by authorities they did not acknowledge. It was argued therefore that the epistemological question about the grounds of claiming p to be true was really a sociological question about the legitimating authorities who say that p is true. Don't examine Hirst's or Peters' arguments, simply look at their social backgrounds and the machinery through which they promote their ideas!

How far do I go along with this radical and relativist criticism of organised knowledge? In so far as the concepts we have are social constructs (they are socially developed ways of organising experience and they change in course of time and from society to society) the validity of what we say would indeed seem relative to the particular social 'agreements' about how to describe experience. It would seem always open to a social group to agree to describe things differently. And the adoption of one description rather than another would, in the last analysis, be a matter of convention. Adolescents, under (if you like) the different 'legitimating authorities' of their peer group, adopt a different way of conceptualising things, reflected very often in a different vocabulary. Hence the frequent breakdown in communication, and the anthropologist-like efforts of some teachers 'to understand' and to 'talk their language'.

However, I want to argue that there are limits within which one can pursue this point. Whatever the conventions whereby we have come to organise experience in one way rather than another, and whatever the different conventional ways by which different groups have come to organise experience, there must be large areas of agreement from which the differences might be explored, alternative views understood and then found more or less adequate. Whatever the differences between me and my fourth formers (and doubtless there are many) and the breakdowns in communication (they just don't know what I mean), let us not underestimate the broad areas of shared experience and shared concepts in so far as we share similar bodily and mental characteristics and communicate through an identifiable language system. Wherever our different interests and trains of thought take us, whatever the different social groups that we find mental sustenance in, we commence and remain in a material world subject to laws of cause and effect in which things such as tables and chairs, activities such as football and memorising, persons such as Deborah and Melody, roles such as teaching and learning, mental happenings such as pain and joy are identified, picked out, and made the basis of communication. There are limits to which one can say we inhabit different realities. That reality has been classified and individuated in the way that it has is in part conventional, but the conventions are shared, and those that are not can be learnt. This is why it is important for teacher and learner to be together a lot, informally as well as in formal teaching situations. Gradually, over a period of time, after constant efforts to know what the other means, understanding takes place, the 'rules' of the others' 'language games' have been mastered.

Secondly, there are limits to how far one can talk about our concepts, our construction of reality, as conventional. It is conceivable that we might not have classified different animals into cats and dogs (just as some pupils may not distinguish between discipline and punishment). But that we can so distinguish has got something to do with cats and dogs, with a world that makes distinctions possible (because it has distinguishable features). And such a real world that makes distinctions possible (whether or not we choose to make those distinctions) includes the social world of people intending, striving, agreeing, and valuing. One may indeed give a sociological account of why we come to make the distinctions we do but there must be something about the world which makes these distinctions possible – even distinctions within (ways of dividing up) the social reality. A child is intelligent or not, certainly, because that is a category we choose to use. But, given our choice of so classifying pupils, he is intelligent or not because of how he behaves, and that is not something we choose.

Thirdly, the limitations of redefining knowledge or the way we see things derive from the very context in which the redefinitions take place. You cannot dismantle and rebuild a ship on the high seas – it must be a bit by bit process. Parts are replaced when old or worn, when they fail in their particular job. Similarly, there is indeed a constant need for conceptual development, as old concepts fail to meet up to new needs. But the redefinition of concepts must take place within a wider context of shared meanings. Otherwise where do the terms of ones redefinition come from, or to whom could one communicate one's new definitions? One must be within a language before one can perceive its defects and thus the places where change and adaptation are required. Again, there is little point in fundamental speculation about morals and religion, about politics and arts, unless one has already entered sympathetically and imaginately into the attempts by others to identify and tackle problems within these areas. This is not to say that no respect should be given to the thoughts and feelings, doubts and questionings of the pupils in these matters. Far from it. My argument constantly is that this is where one must begin – it is these that are to be educated. But to educate them the teacher must be within a worked out tradition from which he can draw strength and inspiration in helping the pupils do better in their thinking. From inside such social activities the teacher can draw upon the conceptual tools, the habits of thinking, the imaginative efforts of a socially developed way of experience in order to provide a more adequate way of thinking for those already, if only embryonically, beginning to move in that direction.

The conventional nature of the way in which we have come to describe experience and to define reality does not warrant the conclusion that anything goes – that any conception of reality promoted by a pupil is as good as another and that the classroom is essentially a market place where meanings are negotiated. This would be to neglect both the very strict logical limits within which one might talk of inhabiting alternative realities and the essentially public nature of the way in which we have come to see things in an ever more refined way.

3. Changing knowledge and changing truth

There is frequently a wrong identification of knowledge with infallibility: that is, it is argued from 'x knows that p' not only that 'p is true', but that 'x could not possibly be mistaken about p'. This wrong identification gives rise to the sceptic's argument that, since there is never ground for certainty (it is always logically possible one might be mistaken), there can be no justifiable knowledge claims. Furthermore, this scepticism would seem justified by the historical changes in every kind of theoretical explanation. Knowledge changes and there is no reason for believing that it will cease to do so.

Two educational conclusions are drawn from this. The first, the more radical, undermines any conception of intellectual authority for, since it is always possible to be wrong, no one has the right to be sure and therefore no one has the right to tell another what is the case or to organise knowledge for the pupil along preordained lines. Teacher and pupil each reconstructs his own reality in his own way, each reconstruction being as good as the other, for there is no firm ground from which one might arbitrate between the two. The second conclusion is less radical but, possibly for that reason, more pernicious: since knowledge is constantly changing, and there is little use in teaching what constitutes knowledge today but not tomorrow, one can ignore the content of knowledge (say, physics) and teach only 'scientific method', or (more vaguely) help the children 'to learn how to learn'. At such a general level of educational aim many curriculum distinctions become irrelevant.

However, neither educational conclusion is warranted by the premises. It is true that in any area of intellectual activity (whether it be ethics, aesthetics, science or mathematics) different ideas, some of far-reaching significance, compete for the allegiance of those who are thinking about the respective problems. It is true, furthermore, that the rules for deciding upon the merits of different explanatory ideas are rarely formulated, for rules are generally made explicit within a theoretical framework and it is precisely the truth of the theoretical framework that is being questioned. But it does not follow from this that the acceptance of one theoretical framework rather than another is a matter of choice, and that there are different definitions of knowledge and different reconstructions of reality which are not open to rational reconciliation. If this were the case, then ideas would no longer have authority – only the power structures, the institutions and the charisma of the persons who told them, and what previously was seen as an exciting battle of ideas would now be no more than an institutional or personal struggle for power. Indeed, the division of the curriculum would represent the success stories in this power struggle, and one way of weakening the power of those in positions of control would be to break down these subject barriers.

To support the view that change in knowledge or in theoretical framework is ultimately a matter of choice, reference is made to Kuhn (1962). Roughly, Kuhn's argument is as follows: firstly, in general, the truth or falsity of a scientific claim is decided by applying the rules and procedures that are constitutive of a particular theory, what Kuhn calls the over-all master theory or paradigm, and this is characteristic of 'normal science'. However, science is characterised by changes in paradigm – 'normal science' gives way to periods of crisis. Therefore, there are in fact different paradigms and each paradigm is, when its full implications have been made explicit, a 'self-contained' conceptual and theoretical system. So, finally, therefore, since truth and falsity are defined within a paradigm, the change from one paradigm to another is a revolution rather than a growth, to be explained empirically or socio-psychologically rather than logically (i.e. in terms of causes rather than reasons). Put simply, some people just come to see things differently. In some cases these differences are far-reaching and the over-all view of things can, in the ultimate analysis, be held not rationally but dogmatically. Kuhn's analysis of scientific change as essentially irrational and revolutionary lends itself to those who, even at a level far removed from that of Newton and Einstein, wish to talk about each person's world view or definition of reality, and thus who see small groups inhabiting 'total ideologies' or individuals in the last resort confined to their solipsistic universes. For is not the concept of truth here simply what is defined as truth within a paradigm? And is not such a paradigm ultimately a matter of arbitrary choice?

78

My criticism of this view is similar to the criticism made in the last section against reducing the way in which we organise and talk about experiences to mere convention. In general terms, the facts do not bear out this analysis. It is always possible to distinguish between the internal and external history of a science. Whatsoever the non-scientific explanations that can be given for changes, these changes can be, and are, appraised by the general principles that are constitutive of science in general or that particular branch of it. This appraisal is logically distinct from a sociological account in that it relies, as a sociological account does not, upon implicit principles of procedure that constitute science. These of course might be very general: the repeated testing against experience, the checking of results with others, the search for possible alternative explanations, the avoidance of inconsistency, the search for comprehensiveness. But they have specific application in that they are procedures for deciding between rival theories that attempt to explain a range of particular problems, and the success of one theory grows out of the failure of another.

Secondly, there are logical reasons why the differences between theories cannot be just convention, for if this were the case there would be no distinction between a correct or an incorrect account of the world. This of course is what some radical educationists would like to say but it is, upon analysis, incoherent. To claim, as the sceptics do, that we are often mistaken and that there is no logical guarantee on any one occasion that we are not mistaken, is to presuppose some idea of a non-mistaken or true account of the world. At least the truth must remain as a conceivable ideal, for otherwise sense could not be attached to 'mistake'. It may be that on any one occasion we can never be fully certain that what we believe is true, but to harbour this possibility presupposes both that one would know what would count as a falsification of a belief in particular circumstances and that the general background of beliefs (about the existence of any external world, other people, etc) is basically correct. Ultimately scientific theories must stand or fall in so far as they describe and predict what can be experienced and, although experience can be conceptualised differently, that does not mean that things can be made to happen simply by a change of concepts. In that sense, therefore, experience does remain 'the impartial arbiter of their (the scientists') controversies' and, given a theoretical framework that governs how we conceptualise experience, any particular report of experience is true or false. It will remain so irrespective of the subsequent abandonment of that theoretical framework because of its inadequacy in meeting new problems that arise. Newtonian mechanics might, as a theoretical system, be superseded for particular purposes but, given this theoretical system, what is said within it is either true or false and will remain so even when the system is superseded since there must be something about the world which made it possible to describe it in this way in the first place.

The sceptic is correct therefore to say that absolute and infallible rational standpoints cannot be found (that knowledge, including the conceptual schemes of logic, mathematics, and the sciences, changes), but the consequence of this is neither scepticism nor ultimate dependence upon dogma or irrational choice, for the change in knowledge is made by appeal to general principles of rationality when existing theory fails in its explanatory purpose, and the recognition of mistakes in any theoretical account presupposes the conceivability of a true account. It would be more accurate to talk of the growth of knowledge rather than its change and, in so far as the success of one theoretical account grows out of the proven failures of a previous one, the change in theory does not warrant that one should no longer teach what is current in theory, even moral theory. One might say that it is the job of the teacher to introduce the pupil to the present state of a disciplined way of enquiring or doing, even if this is to be superseded at some later date, because the pupil would otherwise not grasp the principles of procedure or criticism by which theoretical change takes place, and because the current theoretical account, even if superseded, at least would be the best approximation to the truth.

4. Conclusion

There is no simple way of analysing the activities that should enter into a curriculum. Certainly, despite their variety and possible range, there is a cognitive core to each mental activity which makes it the possible basis of educational development. But when the general characteristics of the cognitive element are themselves analysed – the different kinds of cognition, the reference to standards and to conceptual structures – there is frequently missing that further dimension of the social context in which knowledge is developed and remains rooted.

Such a social context does of course provide opportunity for abuse. The organisations formed to promote both the development and the transmission of knowledge can become the very barriers to people knowing. They can raise walls which only a privileged few are allowed to enter. They can make mysterious and esoteric what is rooted in the thoughts and questionings of each one of us. With a tendency to conservatism such institutional arrangements for promoting learning might disguise important disciplinary changes that take place. Examinations that they foster (for whatever social, and possibly non-educational purpose) might often put a premium on the least significant factors of mental development, and might encourage a spurious kind of education. There is no reason why organisations established to foster education should continue to do so.

For this reason it is important constantly to be subjected to the sort of critique which sociologists are now developing. It is important to be aware of the social context in which knowledge is developed, promoted, made accessible, and in which control by those in authority might be exercised. 'O' and 'A' level results are the *test* of good performance, not what it means to perform well and, as with any other test, they must constantly be examined to check whether they really are testing good performance. Within the school it is important constantly to examine critically the way in which control is exercised over the curriculum, how it is organised, what is taught and by whom.

But, in becoming more sensitive to the possible ways in which knowledge is controlled, one is not forced into the position of saying that the organisation of knowledge is simply a matter of social control, or that a critique of organised knowledge is simply a critique of those who organise and produce it. It is necessary to keep questions about the validity of our different kinds of intellectual activity distinct from questions about their genesis, otherwise the very critique of how we come to organise knowledge is itself unintelligible. There are logical limits to what meanings can be negotiated or realities reconstructed. Meanings that enter into our different mental activities are socially developed, shared, inherited, and transmitted – not negotiated or bargained over by individuals on a day to day basis. And the curriculum in its general concern for mental and thereby cognitive development must provide the means for introducing pupils into the differentiated way in which man has come to think and to act.

On the other hand it is an introduction into a current set of activities, into a way of living, engaged in by different communities of people who share problems, engage in mutual criticism, seek help and inspiration from each other. What pupils are being introduced to is a socially significant way of knowing and acting and not a private world.

Summary
1 A radical criticism of curriculum knowledge is that its divi-

82

sions reflect different power groups and are means of exercising social control. This stress upon the socially constructed nature of disciplined ways of thinking and upon the socially situated nature of acquiring them is important, but (2,3) it would be wrong to argue from it that all truth is relative or that one way of seeing things is as good as another. 4 Nonetheless one should beware of the constant danger of educational justification being submerged beneath the mechanisms of social control or of worthwhile learning becoming an individual, non-cooperative exercise. There is a social dimension both to the organisation and to the process of learning.

Further reading
New directions in sociology of education are found in two collections of essays, Young (1971) and Filmer (1972). Gorbutt and others (1972) provide a useful symposium explaining the new paradigm, applying it critically to a B.Ed. course and raising some of its philosophical difficulties. Different issues of *Radical Education* show its influences upon teachers' thinking about their practice. Whitty (1974) gives an overview of these developments, indicating future trends.

5 RESPECTING COMMONSENSE

1. Commonsense beliefs

A criticism of much school knowledge (implicit especially within the 'new directions in sociological theory') is that it has little respect for the knowledge and know-how that the children bring to school. Indeed, even colleges and institutes of education seem to make little allowance for the thought and the quite extensive experiences of their own students. The assumption is that they are to be introduced to, initiated into, something to which they are as yet outsiders. A lecturer on this view can pursue his preplanned programme (planned without *these* students in view) because, firstly, there is a given body of knowledge to be put across and, secondly, those coming on the course will not yet have had it put across. Fundamental, therefore, to this *dis*respect for the learner's way of thinking is a belief in a radical disconnection between how the pupils or students ordinarily think and how one thinks *after* initiation, after the introduction to a particular form of knowledge or a disciplined mode of enquiry.

A main theme of this book has been the need to respect and attend to the ways of thinking, the reflective experience and the modes of operating of those who are to learn, for it is this – the rich and complex mental life they already have – which is to be educated. They already have a complex scheme of things, a set of beliefs, a style of life, however inadequate in *some* respects and for *certain* purposes we judge it to be. Moreover, I have argued that, in educating these people engaged as they are in this or that form of mental life, one draws upon the resources of different traditions of thought, different established ways of thinking and of acting. The art of teaching lies in bringing the two into contact – the current interests of the pupil and the socially developed traditions of thought and behaviour. The one must be put at the service of the other.

To believe this is incompatible with the total disconnection of the two. The account of education as initiation (see Peters 1966, chapter 2) has served a useful purpose, but it is an exaggeration of the truth which has supported a wrong and alienating view of the curriculum. And such a description becomes paradoxical indeed where what we are being instructed into are forms of knowledge which are the fundamental categories of all truth-seeking activities. Either the initiates have never engaged in thoughtful activity before or they are already on the inside of the different forms of knowledge and thereby do not require initiation.

What I need to do is to explain a little further what I mean by the ordinary, commonsense, but possibly quite sophisticated, way of thinking which the learner brings and which itself is to be refined, cultivated, made more disciplined, systematic and accomplished without necessarily losing its essential character, without necessarily becoming something different in kind. This is by no means easy. The development of the ordinary, unspecialised and undifferentiated thought of the child is what many primary school teachers, and indeed many teachers of English (for there is nothing esoteric about good literature), would doubtless claim to be doing. But the words 'ordinary' and 'commonsense' are slippery ones. What do they mean?

Commonsense very often refers to those beliefs (those explanations and accounts) that seem to be so obvious that they require no justification. Indeed, to say to someone 'It is

85

just commonsense' puts a stopper to further questioning. Commonsense is that range of beliefs which people share and hold in an unquestioning sort of way, and which provide a basic view of the world, of their position within the world, and of how they ought to act. Commonsense therefore is not something which is deliberately learnt although it could be deliberately taught. It is what is picked up from others, deposited in a language maybe (its clichés, its aphorisms), or a kind of folklore, the origins or justification of which are lost (for to require justification is no longer to see it as commonsense). It provides the rules-of-thumb with which each person is able to live, make decisions and engage in various pursuits. And it probably works well enough when the physical and social environments are sufficiently stable for the continued success of unquestioned assumptions.

What, however, is commonsense to one group may not be to another. The black adolescent in a Brixton school might treat as commonsense certain beliefs about this society, which his white counterpart in Richmond would find far from self-evident. But the commonsense beliefs that the child brings to school are not to be disregarded. Far from it, they are the ones which dominate that child's mind most completely and which need to be brought under critical control. It is not the set of beliefs that needs to be rejected, but only (slowly) the manner, the commonsense way with which they are held. The teacher too has many views, securely held as commonsense, that need to be questioned. Possibly the chief benefit from inservice courses lies in the questioning of what was previously unquestioned – the inherited intelligence of one's pupils, the 'traditional' organisation of knowledge, the hierarchy of authority within the school. Hence in talking about commonsense beliefs of particular groups – of these fourth formers, say – one has in mind the unquestioned assumptions of that group through which its members understand themselves and each other, tackle personal problems, pick out certain features of experience as significant – if you like (but with all the qualifications of the last chapter) '*their* reality of everyday life'. And to educate that particular group would involve, over time, increasing the powers of reflection upon and criticism of what previously was adhered to at a purely commonsense level.

There is a further characteristic of our commonsense beliefs which is important to bear in mind. There are certain beliefs which cannot really be questioned; they provide the fundamental framework within which any thinking takes place. I refer to basic beliefs in an external, material world, in which objects interconnect in causal relationships, in which there are other people who can think, feel, and have intentions. These already provide a shared framework between teacher and pupil within which communication is possible and wherein less indisputable beliefs might be questioned. This is most important. The rather mysterious languages of some specialisms (which makes initiation seem the most appropriate metaphor for educational processes) must in some way relate back to the commonsense framework of material objects in space and time and of persons acting thoughtfully and intentionally upon such objects. It is because of this, because the specialist disciplines must be logically connected with the commonsense framework of everyday discourse we all share, that I do not see such a radical disconnection between the language of the pupils (even Deborah) and that of the 'educated man'. Such a disconnection is so often assumed in the philosophy of the curriculum, and creates a gulf between the interests of the pupils and the interests of the school.

2. Commonsense discourse

Two points seem to me to be significant. Firstly, the developed mind is the development of a mind already operating, sometimes very effectively, at a commonsense level. Secondly, the development of that mind through the

87

curriculum achieves something that is more than common-sense, though clearly an extension of it. What that more is has already been hinted at in the last section: commonsense indicates an unquestioning manner with which beliefs are held, and educating someone with *those* beliefs and with *those* ways of understanding requires getting them to reflect more systematically and more critically upon them. A mark of the ill-educated man, no matter how learned he is, is the dogmatic way in which he clings to his beliefs, the invulnerability to criticism of his taken-for-granted world.

The curriculum then should aim at the systematic reflection upon the commonsense beliefs of the pupil and student, and, in doing this, should draw upon those areas of enquiry which have extended the commonsense thinking of mankind into definite traditions of disciplined enquiry.

In what way are such traditions of disciplined thinking different from the commonsense (even sophisticated commonsense) thinking of the learner? Firstly, they have generally, but not always, forged a greater precision in the use of specific concepts. In classical mechanics, for example, 'force' is *quantifiable* relative to mass and the laws of motion. An ideal of the natural sciences would be the replacement of qualitative by quantitative descriptions wherever possible, as for instance in substituting precise standards of measurement for everyday judgements of temperature. Again, even in those areas that do not claim to be quantifiable, greater precision is frequently sought. People are asked to define their terms, to analyse what they mean, to state what logically follows. The religious views held at a commonsense level are rendered more precise (and thus made more open to critical examination) in systematic theology.

But what must never be lost sight of in pointing to this difference between ordinary commonsense ways of thoughtful living and systematic disciplined reflection is that the latter is a reflection upon the former, that the more technically precise use of terms is a refinement for particular purposes of what generally exist (and have a life) in the former, and that the quantification of phenomena typical of the sciences is an abstraction from a qualitatively rich world of ordinary experience. It is ultimately in the commonsense world of ordinary people that the systematically developed and more precise world of the specialist must have reference.

Secondly, the taken-for-granted way in which beliefs are frequently held is itself challenged in the curriculum. The truth of what previously was taken to be self-evident is now questioned, and this raises further issues about the different kinds of truth conditions. This vagueness of truth conditions is what the more systematic reflection of specialist thinking upon commonsense would seek to eliminate, and thus the teacher is able to draw upon those different traditions of thought in which different ways of testing the truth, of deciding between good and bad, valid and invalid, justifiable and unjustifiable, have been made more explicit. Visits to farms by junior children both challenge and inform their beliefs – they might be (if properly conducted) the beginnings of a more reflective, informed set of beliefs, grounded in experience about the sustenance and continuity of life. The fourteen-year-old with beliefs, vague maybe, about his future role in the community, is gradually led into a more questioning attitude towards the grounds upon which these views are held. Certainly the aim would eventually be for the pupil or student to be conscious of the need to verify what he currently holds to be true and to be aware of the different modes of verification in different kinds of discourse. Rarely however could one expect this to be fully achieved in school. It is but an educational ideal towards which one might more or less approximate. The verification must ultimately be related to the world of things and persons which we all, pupil and teacher, inhabit. It is to this shared world of experiences that the verification of even quite narrowly specialised areas of enquiry must relate.

Thirdly, the way we argue at the non-reflective, commonsense level is frequently not very systematic. Hidden assumptions are rarely made explicit. Short-cuts are common because of the large areas of shared meanings and agreed connections within respective groups of people. Theoretical studies have usually attempted to make the steps in argument more clear and more precise. Part of the refinement of commonsense thinking will be the development in the pupil of a capacity to state his reasons, to move logically from one consideration to another, to draw conclusions, to maintain only as firm a belief as the premisses warrant, to distinguish between different kinds of argument for different purposes and problems. Of course, at a very elementary level – at primary school and possibly for much of secondary school for some pupils – the capacity for argument, for reasoning out, may not be highly differentiated. For all that, it will require the disciplining of the mind, the development of certain mental habits and abilities. Only later will it be necessary to show differences in kind of argument and in doing so to draw upon the resources provided by different kinds of subject-matter.

Finally, the commonsense thinking of the child covers such a large area of life, so much that is personal and important. Systematic reflection upon this requires the focusing of attention upon particular areas of concern. It requires a limitation of 'the universe of discourse'. Part of what is meant by a distinct tradition of thought is a particular area of experience picked out by groups of people for special attention and development. It is upon such specialised, limited areas of intensive examination that the well informed teacher might draw to assist the pupil or the student with his, as yet, undifferentiated thoughts about life and its problems. For example, on training or inservice courses for teachers, the tutor must himself be grounded in some distinct universe of discourse from which he can draw strength in helping the students with those educational questions which, as such, cannot be posed within that universe of discourse alone. It would be wrong to see the point of philosophy departments in institutes or colleges to be chiefly in teaching philosophy as such. Rather they should be centres of intellectual strength from which particular teachers might work more effectively in the interdisciplinary framework required by the examination of educational issues. Philosophy is only one universe of discourse and cannot comprehend all the issues of practical thinking entering into educational decisions. For that reason it is a resource to be drawn upon in assisting the intelligent (if only at a commonsense level) thinking of the practising teacher.

Very often the field of discourse is limited to a particular logical kind of entity which might be a purely theoretical construct (such as 'particles' in physics) or an artificially restricted conception of some object (such as 'the rational man' in economics). A theoretically developed mode of discourse therefore often restricts itself to a technically defined type of individual. And these individuals are not necessarily the things, persons, or events identified in commonsense discourse. But although they are not necessarily the same the specialised entities must be related to the points of reference of commonsense. *Homo Skinnerius,* like *homo economicus,* is an abstraction from the rather complex being we meet on the street or in literature.

The teacher of physics therefore is not introducing the pupils to a radically different world, a completely alien way of looking at things. Certainly the world of particles must seem to the beginner to be one such different world, but it must be logically connected with the world of tables and chairs (just as the psychological world of unconscious drives must be connected with Johnny's observed behaviour and with our ordinary ways of assessing motivation). And one is forced into this more theoretical universe of discourse because of the inadequacies beyond certain points of our ordinary ways of thinking about these matters. Of course, if you begin physics with 'atoms', 'particles' and 'molecules'

91

then there will be a radical disconnection between ordinary and specialist ways of thinking that leads to mystification and ultimately alienation. But this need not be the way to begin.

Theoretical discourse therefore abstracts from our commonsense perception of things for specific purposes, stipulates a tighter conceptualising of experience, makes stricter logical demands than are present in our normal reflection upon concrete experience, and constructs new individuals. But such abstraction, stipulation and construction starts from the commonsense world of things and persons, and returns to it for its relevance and application.

To say, however, that theoretical and more disciplined thinking returns to ordinary language for its application does itself raise problems for commonsense. Might not competent theoreticians simply lack the ability to apply theory to practice? Thus the expert in learning theory fails to apply his theoretical insights to his own teaching about learning theory; the student of ethics cannot recognise his own moral failings; an army of economic theorists can't make an economy work, and the theorist in administrative practice lives in a state of practical confusion. What one says of such people, proven and certificated though they are in their own theoretical field, is that they 'lack judgement', they have no commonsense. Hence commonsense has this further dimension: the man of commonsense is a 'man of judgement', the master of certain practical arts. And it is the job of the school, or of any educational agency, to increase such practical powers of the mind, for without it (without the capacity to relate theory to practice) there seems little point in the theory.

3. Commonsense judgement

We recently had a foreign student staying in our house. He wanted to talk about Descartes, the French mind [sic], the

English mind (in so far as he believed we had one), the Common Market and the nature of science. But he could not boil an egg; he burnt the element on our electric kettle at his first attempt to make coffee; he was unable to cope with a four-year-old giving him a goodnight kiss, and he was unable without help to keep himself clean. The continuation of studies into his middle twenties was only one aspect of his inability to face up to the practical tasks of living. He had no practical judgement, no practical commonsense, and this showed a serious deficiency in education, however articulate he might have proved to be about the *Discourse on Method*.

In talking about a man of commonsense, one is concerned with abilities rather than beliefs – the ability to make appropriate practical judgements or to relate theory to the concrete situation or to apply principles to practice. He knows how to cope with practical situations, and to apply his theory. The man of commonsense has an indefinable quality called judgement, and its exercise is an art or skill rather than something which can be theoretically formulated. The man of commonsense lives up to certain standards of behaviour connected with meeting everyday problems. To boil an empty kettle, to talk about Descartes at breakfast time, to leap at sixteen for the first job that offers good money, shows lack of commonsense and blindness to features which are both obvious and relevant. And school education should be as much concerned with developing the art of practical judgement as it is with achieving academic success – especially in those who (it is easy to detect) need a little prompting. To acquire an art (for that is what commonsense judgement is) cannot result from following a textbook or a set of rules. An art is more than a skill. But like a skill it requires opportunity and practice. A teacher who knows his pupils well can soon discover those who have been so protected or so overwhelmed that they have never acquired the ability to look after themselves, to face up to life's demands or assume responsibility for making choices. Opportunity is needed then, through the life of the school, to help them assume such responsibility. There are limits however to the degree to which the school can assume responsibility for practical and commonsense education of the child.

In fact, at times the school or college seems in this respect counterproductive, and maybe the best educational advice that even an academically successful student might be given is that of leaving full-time study to learn the practical art of living. Where, however, the school can assume greater responsibility is in showing the need to apply theory to practice and to develop the art of connecting the one to the other. Is it not true that very often the theoretically able is lost when put in the everyday world in which the theoretical questions first arose and to which, if they have any validity whatsoever, they must apply? I have known lecturers in learning theory unable to see the connection between their theory and their teaching methods. I know of experts in child development who are at a loss as to how to rear their own children. The reason for this lies, I believe, in what I said in chapter 2: 'knowledge that' has been cut off from the 'knowledge how' upon which it is a systematic reflection. The curriculum has become academic. It has lost its roots in the often practical world with its practical problems and perplexities which generated the more systematic, theoretical investigation in the first place. Theory is of little use without the judgement to recognise the concrete cases to which it is applicable.

4. Conclusion
There is much talk but little written about the commonsense understandings which children bring with them to school, and yet it is these understandings which, more than any other, will form the child's world view and the decisions by which he will determine what to do. It is these therefore which need above all to be educated.

Priority should be given therefore on any school programme to finding out what this commonsense level of operating is. Otherwise the curriculum will leave the pupil very much as he is. And if finding this out requires a more flexible timetable and less time given to more exact, more specialised areas of activity, then such a price must be paid, for otherwise the official programme of the school will have little to say to this or to that pupil.

To find out or to respect such commonsense understandings does not mean however an acceptance either of their content or of the unquestioning manner with which they are held. The first stage in educating *these* pupils with *these* beliefs and *these* ways of thinking will be to get them to reflect critically upon their beliefs and hidden assumptions. For them to do this will require the development of mental habits and capacities – to question, to seek out evidence, to respect the views and criticisms of others, to clarify and to articulate – which are not the exclusive possession of any one recognised subject area. The beginnings of education, the gaining of a critical and questioning mind, need not be within a subject based curriculum. Certain kinds of curriculum activity might however be more successful than others in developing interest and forming a reflective attitude. I have found very simple personality tests and optical illusions good ways of raising intelligent and questioning interest in children's otherwise unquestioning assumptions about their own identity and others' personalities. This could go on under the subject heading psychology. But why should it? It would be only one way in which a teacher could encourage the sort of questioning which, with prompting, might develop into a more systematic and theoretical study. Or again activities such as community service provide the opportunity (if utilised by the teacher) for challenging and making explicit assumptions about one's local society. The *educational* value of such activities would lie in the degree of reflection which arose from them or from the guidance and promptings of the teacher. Doing good works, however virtuous, *may* not be of

95

educational value. Nor will talking about one's works be of educational value unless such talk is reflective, re-ordering the beliefs and assumptions and values as a result of the experience, and trying to make clear the new puzzles and problems that have arisen.

Such critical reflection, then, must soon draw the pupil into areas in which there is already a tradition of answering and coping with such questions. The furtherance by the teacher of the pupil's incipient interest in his personality will require some roots, however short, in those areas of psychology which will provide the tests, the information, the stimulus that will lead on to further development of the pupil's reflection. The expert in a subject area is less in need of preplanning his teaching programme precisely because he has the intellectual resources within him and can thus afford to be more flexible in his approach. He can see the possibilities and the culs-de-sac in different lines of enquiry. Although, therefore, on the one hand I am arguing for a more flexible, more open curriculum, I have no doubt that the teachers on such a curriculum must represent disciplined areas of enquiry which can be both a resource for the questioning pupil and an ideal to which he might aspire.

The aim of teaching here must be eventually to get the child onto the inside of the disciplinary ideal – the systematic attempt to pursue certain questions as far as they will go – and at the same time to equip him with the tools (the skills, the command of literature, the concepts) without which the questioning will flag. If social studies have any validity at all they will have something to say to the pupil puzzled by the isolation of old people met through Task Force or bewildered by the magnitude of the hospital in which he is spending Friday afternoons. Unless these puzzles and these bewilderments become the focal core of community service courses, these will (whatever else they claim in justification) not be educative.

There is however one area of possible misunderstanding.

Some readers may say 'that is all very well but you remain at too general a level. Tell us what these interests are, what these commonsense understandings are, that need to be educated. Then we might be able to prepare ourselves to challenge and to educate them'. Such a question however misses the point. No textbook can say how adolescents in general think or what the captivating interests of the junior child will be. There is no substitute for observing Mary or John at work and play. Indeed, even that is not enough. For what they are interested in, how they understand things, the meanings and values which they attribute to events is not open to observation as such. John spends his time kicking a tennis ball around the street and so (his parents judge) he is interested in football. They then kit him out and present him with a new ball. But was he really interested in football in the same way that his parents understood it? Possibly he enjoyed the domination over the other, smaller children in the street and kicking the ball was but the occasion for achieving this. Possibly it was his way of escaping from the boredom of home or for gaining friends – but other ways would have done just as well. There is no alternative to finding out the interests and the commonsense understandings of children than by getting to know them, observing them, interpreting one's observations, and tentatively testing out one's interpretations. There is no textbook answer, no course that will short-cut the answers. Hence the educational disaster of so many child-centred courses, supposedly based on the interests of the child, that have not got the child's interests or the child's ways of thinking in mind.

Summary

1, 2 Since I have constantly insisted upon respect for the ordinary commonsense language, beliefs, and discourse of the pupils, it has been necessary here to say more about these. Such beliefs are roughly speaking taken for granted and non-reflective; such discourse is unsystematic and imprecise. To educate people operating mainly on the commonsense level requires getting them to reflect upon and to criticise what previously was taken for granted. It requires rendering more precise, systematic and disciplined their commonsense discourse. The public traditions of thought have arisen from such systematic, disciplined reflection and criticism, and should be seen as resources from which the student-centred curriculum draws. 3 Practical thinking is a little different. It is an indefinable quality often neglected in the academically oriented curriculum, and yet without it academic success is of little value. 4 Hence our curriculum principles are now taking shape: a more flexible arrangement than the normal subject based curriculum takes priority in which getting to know the pupil and extending his commonsense ways of thinking and acting are the important things.

Further reading
Commonsense has received very little theoretical examination from philosophers of education, despite its central importance to teaching. An exception is Perry (1965) and Whitehead (1932, passim), and the continuity between theory and practice and between everyday and expert thinking is a constant theme in Dewey (1916).

6 INTEGRATING THE CURRICULUM

1. What it is and what it is not

The integrated curriculum is now a 'fact of life'. The primary school has its integrated day. The new middle school (if we are to believe the Schools Council Working Papers Nos 22 and 42) will be integrating what were previously distinct subjects, especially in the humanities. Recent developments in secondary school curricula stem in part from a distrust of the fragmentary nature of the traditional, subject divided curriculum. And in the training of teachers special provision is made (particularly in the junior secondary courses) to prepare students for a more integrated approach.

However, what are frequently referred to as integrated curricula seem to have little in common other than their opposition to the 'disintegration' of the curriculum into distinct, unrelated subjects. And what lies behind this opposition is a wide range of practical difficulties and theoretical ideas. The integrated curriculum both means, and is in organisation, many different things. It is important therefore to ask in integrating the curriculum *what* is being integrated (all subject-matter or only some?), *how* it is being integrated (through a particular theme or topic, a central subject, or the pupil's own enquiry?), and *why* one is wanting to integrate (to provide a more flexible arrangement or because of some deep seated belief about the unity of knowledge?).

My purpose then is to try to find some order in all this, to uncover some of the various principles that underlie different recommendations and, in doing so critically, to indicate a little further the shape of the curriculum I would wish to see.

A useful way to begin (before one seeks to find some coherence in or classification of the many different claims for an integrated curriculum) is to list almost at random the sorts of criticism levelled against a curriculum that is fragmented into isolated teaching units of distinct subject-matters, and thus the sorts of problem that a more integrated curriculum is intended to meet. It often is the case that one understands what a person means by understanding the kind of problem that is worrying him. What is meant by an integrated curriculum depends partly upon the nature of the problems that it is aimed to meet.

Amongst the many criticisms of a subject based curriculum would be:

(a) Insufficient account taken of the pupils' previous experience, levels of understanding, individual perception of things.

(b) Insufficient account taken of the interests of the pupils which could be the focal point of an educational programme.

(c) Failure to link the pastoral care of the school with curriculum activities – i.e. too clear a demarcation between caring for the pupil as a person and developing the pupil's mind.

(d) Inhibition of close personal relations between teacher and pupil, thought necessary by some if the teacher is to help the individual pupil and the pupil to trust the teacher.

(e) Termination of worthwhile enquiries because they cannot be confined within the boundaries of subject areas.

(f) Learning difficulties arising from the constant switch of attention from one subject-matter to another.

100

(g) Inability to accommodate practical and interdisciplinary concerns such as careers advice, sex education or current affairs.

(h) Links between subject-matters not taught, and support of one subject by another not provided.

(i) Inflexibility of organisation – both of time and of space – so that desirable educational activities (e.g. outside visits) cannot be pursued.

(j) Too sudden transition from primary to secondary modes of operating.

(k) The pupil's initiative in his own studies discouraged.

Such a list is random and incomplete, but doubtless readers will find such a list strikes one or two familiar chords. One should note that some of these objections are levelled solely against the *organisation* of the subject based curriculum and not against the subjects themselves. For example, one might believe that field work is an important part of biological or historical studies, but often made impractical by a curriculum divided into small subject units. Especially in such a 'rich' environment as Inner London social studies could become the informed and systematic reflection upon the social environment within and outside the school. But this becomes practically impossible if it is timetabled for one double period per week.

Nonetheless, despite the integrated curriculum being in some cases a purely organisational device for dealing with a subject based curriculum in a more flexible and effective way, this is by no means generally the case. There are, underlying the proposals to integrate, different principles not only of organisation but of educational rationale, and these (as I have argued in detail elsewhere (Pring 1971)) reflect important differences in theory about the nature of knowledge.

A good summary of the misgivings felt about a subject based curriculum is given in the Schools Council Working Paper No 36, *Religious Education in Secondary Schools,* although the basis and the validity of these misgivings are not given.

According to the working paper:

> In recent years there has been a cautious movement in
> secondary schools away from the old 'fragmented' type of
> curriculum towards a 'holistic' approach. This movement
> was given considerable support by the central position
> given to it by some writers in a number of working papers
> and reports from Schools Council projects and from Sub-
> ject Committees. The proposal to raise the school-leaving
> age provided a stimulus for a reappraisal of the secondary
> school curriculum. In particular, attention has been
> directed to the problem of counteracting the apathy of
> pupils who will not take any public examination but will
> be required to spend an additional year in school. By
> concentrating on the interests and needs of these early
> leavers, it became apparent that subject divisions in the
> time-table were an artificial restriction. They either
> divided learning into a series of unrelated and not very
> relevant units, or made for a great deal of duplication of
> subject-matter. It was decided to select themes relevant to
> the pupils and to investigate them from the points of view
> of a number of subjects grouped under the general heading
> of the 'humanities' – geography, history, literature, the
> arts, and religious education and to link some of these with
> some of the natural sciences or the social sciences, and
> many different types of 'combined studies', 'integrated
> studies', 'social studies', 'general studies' and 'related
> studies' are to be found in secondary schools today.

Misgivings here, as elsewhere, are reflected in the way in
which the paper described a subject based curriculum as
fragmented, apathy-inducing, artificially restricting, unrelated, irrelevant, duplicating. And there is a general (and at
the moment still vague) idea that such misgivings would be
overcome by (i) explicitly linking things together, (ii) planning things as a whole, (iii) concentrating on the needs and

102

interests of the children, (iv) selecting relevant themes.

We are accustomed in secondary schools (and to some extent in primary schools) to a curriculum divided into different subjects not related to each other and taught quite independently. I have already indicated the difficulties in organising the curriculum in this way. Some are of a philosophical sort (as, for example, those argued in chapters 3,4 and 5); others arise more from the learning and administrative consequences of the practice of a subject based curriculum. 'Integrated curriculum' is an imprecise term that covers a range of curriculum responses to these difficulties. In the following sections I shall distinguish four such kinds of curriculum response. In doing so I shall draw to some extent upon the analysis I gave of integration in the Open University course E203, *Curriculum Design and Development* (see Pring 1976). You should refer to that for a more detailed account and for a development of the practical implications.

2. Integration in correlating distinct subject-matters

An integrated curriculum might well find acceptable the analysis of subject-matter given in chapter 2. Economists might stick to economics, historians to history, but the one might wish to use the subject-matter taught by the other and make curriculum arrangements accordingly. The historian may find aspects of the industrial revolution easier to explain if the advantages of specialisation of labour have been taught in economics. The literary qualities of the nineteenth century novel will be more easily taught if one can assume historical acquaintance with the period. An integrated curriculum, in being a response to this kind of teaching problem, would be a matter of creating connections between subjects.

Such correlation might involve questions of a very tricky kind:

. . . not simply organisational questions, but logical questions about the relation of one subject-matter to another. For example, what mathematical knowledge enters into, and is necessarily presupposed by, Nuffield 'A' level biology? What economic understanding is required for a proper historical grasp of the 'agricultural revolution'? What technological knowledge is required for an understanding of urbanisation, etc?

Behind this notion of integration is the belief that there are logically distinct subject-matters, and that these distinctions need to be respected in planning a curriculum. Nonetheless, there is also the realisation that certain kinds of knowledge presuppose others of a different kind, and that there is a need, in designing a curriculum, to work out what presupposes what.

Personally I find the arguments for this correlation of distinct subject areas compelling. Even where one is firmly convinced of the autonomous nature of different disciplines of enquiry, it cannot be doubted that one subject area frequently uses the 'material' of another (or makes assumptions about understandings within another). In retrospect I can say that at school my own historical grasp of what was happening in 19th century England was sadly deficient because of my technological ignorance. (Pring 1976, Unit 12)

3. Integration through themes, topics or ideas

Often themes, topics or ideas are said to provide the integrating element within a curriculum. They are explored in an interdisciplinary manner and, in the exploration, disciplinary differences become blurred and possibly unrecognisable.

Bernstein (1967) expresses this in the following way: 'When the basis of the curriculum is an idea which is supra-subject, and which governs the relationship between subjects, a number of consequences may follow. The subject is no longer dominant, but subordinate to the idea which governs a particular form of integration'.

Possibly the most interesting attempt to explore the curriculum possibilities of this idea is to be found in the Schools Council Integrated Studies Project. According to their handbook (Keele 1972), the project 'examined the problems and possibilities of integrated studies in the "humanities" area of the curriculum'. Subject areas to be integrated were to be the social sciences and the expressive arts, but clearly contributions would be required from other areas too. The purpose of seeking greater integration was, firstly, to organise learning so that otherwise distinct disciplines would be related, secondly, to relate knowledge more closely to the personal concerns of the learner and, thirdly, to make possible the exploration of large and complex human issues, which of course rarely confine themselves within the limits of logically distinct subject areas. In pursuing this threefold purpose the team chose a thematic approach and developed six curriculum units illustrative of this.

It is not my purpose here to look critically at that project. Indeed criticism of any project requires close examination of what happens in practice and not just of the attempt by the team to make explicit the thinking which entered into their organisation of practice. But the project illustrates the different strands of thinking which enter into proposals to integrate the curriculum around themes, topics or ideas – and such different strands of thinking are reflected in the different practices to be observed in schools that have adopted themes rather than subjects as units of organisation.

In the first place themes, far from supplanting the notion of distinct disciplines, *sometimes* presuppose them. They are ways of showing how different disciplines interconnect in the pursuit of particular questions, and the type of integration taking place is very similar to that described in the last section.

105

Secondly, however, where this is not the purpose, they are seen as an alternative way of structuring thought. The integrating idea (e.g. 'power') is somehow supra-subject. The subject is in some sense subordinate to the idea. There are overarching ideas which need to be explored – overarching in the sense that they cannot be confined within the boundaries of any one subject area and yet are crucial structuring elements in our thinking.

Thirdly, themes or topics sometimes signify important issues which are worthy of study in their own right, whether or not they display the interconnection of disciplines. To make such themes the part basis of organising a curriculum does not necessarily challenge the view so far argued in this book that there are distinct kinds of subject-matter, different kinds of knowledge, upon which a curriculum must draw and to which the pupil needs to be introduced. It simply says that in addition attention should be given to certain interdisciplinary questions because they are important. Of course, it does raise the question for the teacher or curriculum planner of how one comes to select certain themes as more important than others. The relatively trivial nature of many themes chosen by schools (e.g. dinosaurs, eskimos) would indicate that it is not the need to study complex human issues which is usually the reason for integration.

A theme based curriculum, therefore, is an alternative way of organising the curriculum – alternative to a curriculum based upon distinct subject-matters. But, unless its rationale is similar to that in the last section, it would need to show how a theme or idea or topic can itself provide a structure to the way in which the pupil is to learn how to think. It would need to show how, by mastering the idea of 'power', for example, the pupil would be introduced to a distinctive way of structuring his thinking, how his mind would in some way be developed and be made more effective. But it is this kind of reasoning behind or justification of a theme based curriculum which I believe mistaken.

106

I once heard a headmaster of a primary school describe the integration of the curriculum around the idea of bees. Thus there are queen bees, worker bees, and drones. Queen bees introduced the further ideas of royal family, sovereignty, etc; worker bees introduced ideas such as careers, jobs, industriousness; drones introduced ideas about social security, layabouts, and hippies. In this way otherwise distinct tracks of thought were brought together in a new unity. But of course no unified *structure* to thought was given by this or other similar instances of a curriculum integrated around ideas or themes. Rather this was nothing more than the idiosyncratic association of ideas of one particular teacher. There was no conceptual unity, no distinctive way of thinking or enquiring, no publicly developed mode of awareness. One objection I have to many examples of integrated curricula is that they have frequently substituted an individual's structuring of reality, that has not withstood the test of time or of public criticism, for a socially developed mode of thinking that has already been found adequate and has withstood scrutiny by others. The teacher is the mediator of public traditions of awareness and performance in so far as these traditions are relevant to the already active minds of the pupils.

The point is that a word or a concept cannot by itself structure or integrate the thinking of a child; words make sense only within a language and concepts have meaning only within a way of thinking characterised, as I explained before, by a range of concepts, a way of proceeding and a way of testing the truth or validity of what is said. To admit this is to return once again to logically distinct subject-matters. A word, idea or concept therefore cannot provide the structural requirements for organising the curriculum. To make 'transport' the theme to be studied this week or this term does not make sense. What is to be studied, what is to be enquired into, depends not on a title but upon the questions being asked about transport, and either these questions will locate the enquiry in different subject areas or they will (because of their interdisciplinary nature) require the understandings and skills developed within more than one subject area. This set of questions (the problems) are what provide structure, not a theme title, topic or idea.

The justification for integrating the curriculum around themes then is confused, though some justifications do seem plausible. Firstly, 'theme' is sometimes another, possibly misleading way of talking about pupil-initiated learning. It is the pupil's own enquiry that becomes the integrating element. That however gives rise to a different notion of integrated curriculum in terms both of its organisation and of its rationale. This I shall examine in section 5. Secondly, themes sometimes pick out a range of questions, usually of a fairly practical nature, or a range of loosely connected interests and activities, which need to be provided for and which integrate different disciplinary interests. 'Themes' again seems a misnomer, but that does not matter so long as we are aware of these distinctions and the different questions that such distinctions raise.

4. Integration in practical thinking

To talk of an integrated curriculum might not mean an integration of the whole curriculum. There are areas of practical thinking which do not fit into traditional subject areas or into well defined subject-matters. For example, sex education may be seen as a curriculum concern and yet the questions raised will not fit within any one subject-matter. The Humanities Curriculum Project (see Stenhouse 1968) defined certain 'areas of practical living' where contributions from different disciplines must be called upon to aid enquiry. Integration was not explicitly sought, but the resolution of difficulties identified and enquired into by the pupil would demand a personal integration on the basis of multi-disciplinary evidence and argument. The project was given

108

the remit to offer to schools and teachers 'stimulus, support, and materials' for mounting enquiry based courses which cross subject boundaries, especially within the humanities. But this remit was interpreted in a particular way. The purpose of the humanities was taken as the study of human behaviour and experience with a view to enhancing 'understanding and judgement in those areas of practical living which involve complex considerations of values and cultural traditions'.

Hence there are areas of practical living (e.g. relations between the sexes, living in a multi-racial society, making sense of violence and war, living within a democracy) which require understanding and judgement from the pupil, and these in their turn involve evidence and argument from many different subject areas and at the same time bringing them to bear on particular practical questions. Each pupil must learn to be a responsible decision maker within different areas of practical living and this art and the development of this responsibility require curriculum time. Hence essential features of this curriculum programme are (i) multi-disciplinary (ii) enquiry (iii) into important and controversial issues (iv) on the basis of evidence (v) in areas of practical living. The practical resolution of issues by each pupil is the integrating element.

An interesting feature of this project is the integrative role attributed to practical thinking. Practical thinking does involve both value and factual issues. Decisions about moral behaviour require a very complex working out and putting together of general principles of conduct, ordinary matters of fact and theoretical understandings of the situation. Pupils need to be educated about their personal concerns – that is, helped to think more intelligently and imaginatively about them. But such educating cannot be fitted into particular subject areas or indeed into small units timetabled for that purpose. They are broader in scope than any organised branch of knowledge. Furthermore it is often only in relation

109

to such personal and practical concerns that different kinds of enquiry have significances for the pupil.

5. Integration in the learner's own interested enquiry

'Enquiry' is a very general term and it does include a wide range of different activities. One main task of any subject specialist is to teach the methods of enquiry appropriate to a particular subject-matter. There is however an important tradition, described in chapter 3, which stresses the pupils' own enquiry as such, into whatever areas of interest, as the integrating factor in the curriculum. On this view all enquiry is basically of the same kind, and we should be encouraging the pupil to acquire those powers of mind, those habits of thinking, those skill of enquiry which are common to all intellectual pursuits and which give unity to thinking, irrespective of the conventional distinctions thrown up by subject boundaries. It is the personal enquiry of each pupil which is the integrating element, and the teacher therefore must help, encourage, and further that.

The important point for my present purposes lies in the way in which the pursuit by the pupil of his own valued interest, and (where possible) of pupil-initiated learning, might become the focal point of curriculum organisation. It would be the pursuit of this interested enquiry (fitting neatly into no preconceived, teacher planned, categories or subjects) which *for the pupil* integrated his work in school and provided the context in which questions were raised, new facts brought to light, otherwise disconnected experiences brought into relation, skills developed, and experience constantly reconstructed.

There is, within the child-centred tradition, a respect for enquiry as such, especially the enquiry arising from the pupils' own felt interests, as though this is worth encouraging because there are certain generalisable skills, attitudes, and mental powers which characterise all enquiry and are not to be identified with or confined to particular subject-matters. Furthermore it is frequently argued, especially at the primary school, that it is these general characteristics of enquiry that one should foster through project and similar work. Both the philosophical roots and the criticism of the position I have developed already in chapter 3.

6. Conclusion

An integrated curriculum means different things to different people. It reflects in each case, however, the difficulties that people find in a curriculum split up into distinct and frequently unrelated subject-matters. Some of these difficulties are of a purely practical and organisational kind: the need for a more flexible organisational approach in order to accommodate a wider variety of educational experience, teaching strategies and learning opportunities. Why should one assume, as it is assumed in timetables divided up into periods assigned to different subjects, that the pupil always learns best in short bursts? Certainly I do not learn best in such a framework, but we very often assume that pupils do, irrespective of the kind of educational activity they are engaged in.

However, there is generally more to integrated curricula than the provision of a more flexible timetable arrangement. They represent different educational rationales – different educational ideas rooted very often in philosophical views about the nature of knowledge. I have pointed to four: logical interconnection between different kinds of knowledge, the structuring of knowledge around themes, the integration of knowledge in practical thinking, and the integration in enquiry.

My constant argument in this book has been that a curriculum should seek to provide the meeting place between the already active, therefore educable, minds of the pupils and the teachers who represent living traditions of thought that are relevant to the pupils' concerns and interests. To be such a meeting place it must be arranged much more flexibly than is generally the case in secondary schools, for there must be place and scope for the pupil to develop and reveal those concerns and interests which are to be the focus of the teacher's educative activity. Too much organisation and preplanning, too much preconception of what will take place, cannot be educative because it cannot have *these* pupils in mind. Hence, if such openness and flexibility is what people mean by integration, then a more integrated curriculum is what I favour.

More however than this is required, for preparation and therefore planning are necessary, resources do need to be obtained, cooperation between teachers is needed. Firstly, there is a need for different foci of curriculum organisation. There are well defined areas of subject-matter that require systematic treatment – in various aspects of mathematics, in several scientific subjects, and indeed in any disciplined area of activity once this is to be embarked upon by the pupil. The mastery of a disciplined way of thinking and performing requires systematic learning and practising, and the concentration of teaching and material resources.

Secondly, though, no matter how firm one's adherence to the view that knowledge is differentiated into distinct kinds (differences which must be respected in the systematic development of the mind) there are good educational reasons for alternative foci of organisation within the same curriculum, viz. (i) interdisciplinary areas especially of practical living which can be engaged with often in a fairly open-ended way and indeed in a partly practical way, and (ii) individual interests and enquiries that the pupil wishes to pursue that are of significance to him and that, through pursuit, assist the development of the pupil's mind in the acquisition of mental qualities and abilities.

Such further foci of curriculum structure make particular organisational demands: greater flexibility such as block timetabling and block spacing; more collaborative planning, teaching, and reflection as part of the official programme of the school; the creation of resource centres within the school with easy access for pupils and teachers; links with the richer but frequently untapped resources of the local community; tutorial arrangements within the more flexible curriculum that enable a closer knowledge of the pupils' concerns and interests which are, after all, what are to be educated.

This, you might say, is still too vague. One flaw remains in my argument. I have constantly fought shy of saying more exactly what should be the content of such a curriculum – what should be the particular subject-matters, the particular areas of disciplined activity that should be mediated to the pupils. Even if more consideration was given in curriculum planning to the concerns and interests of the pupils, surely, you might say, there must be some idea of those subject-matters which are at the centre of any development of mind and which (whatever the variations) should be on the curriculum.

This I shall attempt to tackle in the next chapter. In criticising Hirst and Phenix I have admitted into the list of possible subject-matters not six realms of meaning or seven forms of knowledge but an indefinite number. How, from such a wide range of possibilities, does one come to make a selection?

Summary

1 I have argued that the curriculum is the meeting place of the already active minds of the pupils with teaching resources that draw upon various public traditions of thought and behaviour. This however requires more flexibility than the subject based curriculum normally permits, thus indicating the need for a more integrated curriculum. But there are different rationales to be discerned behind the move to integration, and (2,3,4,5) I distinguish four – one of

113

which (the theme based curriculum) is misconceived despite its current popularity.

Further reading
Walton (1971) and Warwick (1973) have useful articles about and examples of attempts to integrate the curriculum. James (1968) argues for more interdisciplinary enquiry (I.D.E.). Pring (1971) gives the philosophical basis of different kinds of integration and (1976) indicates what such different ideas imply for practice.

7 CURRICULUM CONTENT

In this chapter I shall try to bring together the various strands of thought developed in the preceding chapters, and show how they point to a certain kind of curriculum organisation and to certain principles for the selection of content. Of course I cannot lay down what precisely should be the content of the curriculum, because a main feature of my argument has been the need to focus the curriculum upon the already active mental life of particular individuals. Without knowing these individuals and the particular context in which they are to be educated I cannot say what should be the content of *their* education (in saying this however I deviate a great deal from much existing theorising about the curriculum).

1. Private interests and public traditions

Firstly, the recipients of any planned educational process are already equipped with tools of thought which enable them to think, question, puzzle, criticise and doubt. By the age of five a child has generally mastered not only very complex rules of grammar and syntax (even if the vocabulary is limited) but also a variety of speech functions (commanding, questioning, gaining attention, exercising social control, explaining, describing and so on). By learning the English language, he has mastered a complex and fruitful way of organising experience, of communicating with others, of entering into various forms of life, and of having an effect upon the physical and social environment. It is this already active mental life, with its ways of judging, classifying and evaluating, that is both the starting-point and the object of any educational process. To bypass this (as so many pre-planned and programmed courses must do) is to stick on the frills of education but to leave the mind basically as it was before. The strength of the child-centred tradition of Dewey and Kilpatrick lay in its recognition of this fact. To put stress upon the interests of the child, not just as the starting-point of the educational process but as the very 'things' that need to be educated, is to point to the individual's ways of thinking and judging as the matter upon which the educator is to work.

On the other hand, I wish to maintain that what I, as a teacher, bring to such active minds is a way of thinking, perceiving or experiencing which assists them in what they are doing or might want to do, which renders even more effective, pleasurable and imaginative what they are already engaged upon. And such a way of thinking is located in various traditions of thought and activity, various modes of experiencing, in which I, as a teacher, am already deeply involved. From my involvement with and mastery of disciplined ways of enquiring, thinking and behaving, I have something relevant and worthwhile to offer the pupils in the very mental preoccupations that already engage them. The teacher of English or the general teacher in the primary school should already be immersed in literary traditions from which stories, texts, descriptions, might be drawn for the benefit of children who think as they do at that age and in that place. And this is as true of an infant seeking a bedtime story as it is a sixteen-year-old preoccupied with metaphysical doubts!

The teacher of philosophy in a course on educational

theory should himself be so involved in the issues, so practised in the arguments, so alert to the perennial problems, that he is able to provide a systematic and coherent challenge to prevailing assumptions. It need not be labelled philosophy. Indeed even he, let alone the students, may not recognise what he is doing at that moment as philosophy. The important thing is that the resources he is offering as a teacher are chiefly the modes of reflection and criticism that he has gained from his own training in a particular social group with a shared and publicly developed tradition of criticism and enquiry. Gradually over a long period it is hoped that the consciousness of his students will be transformed in some respect – will have gained from being in contact with this mode of searching and enquiring. Only some students may come to be fairly self-consciously aware of what they are doing. But does that matter? One is trying to get students to think a little more philosophically about educational issues, not to think philosophically about philosophy. (I am sceptical of the value of separate courses in philosophy, sociology, psychology, and history at initial training level. What is required is systematic reflection upon the know-how of practice, conducted by lecturers and teachers who, first, have shared that practice – they know what is of concern to the students – and who, secondly, have between them different disciplinary resources to put at the disposal of the questioning student. I see little value for the intelligent practitioners to be able to distinguish consciously between philosophical and sociological questions. On the other hand I would resent psychology or sociology or philosophy alone being the teaching resource for helping the student to reflect systematically about that practice.)

Hence, although I seek a loosening of the curriculum bonds in order that greater respect and allowance may be given to the interests and concerns of the pupil or student, I in no way wish to devalue the public traditions of thought, the disciplined modes of enquiry. Rather I argue that such

117

disciplined ways of thinking must characterise *the teacher* and be transferred to the pupil through his critical and challenging communication with him and in the joint attempt to grapple with the pupils' concerns. Such disciplined ways of thinking cannot be imposed by a timetable. Unless a discipline is taught by someone who is himself deeply involved within it, and himself nourished and sustained by it, there is little point in having it taught within the school. A teacher of history who is himself in no way constantly transformed by historical reading and research will have nothing to communicate to the pupils. He will simply underline to them the worthlessness of the subject. Is this not the reason why so much schooling is miseducative? In pursuit of a wide, 'liberal' education, pupils frequently learn one thing only, namely, the irrelevance of what is officially recognised as education to what really concerns them.

Two objections might be raised to this. One, that it is impossible to organise the kind of framework in which the variety of pupil concerns might be matched with a range of teacher resources, and in which therefore such an educative conversation as I have described might take place. Two, that a stage very quickly arrives when systematic involvement with a limited universe of discourse becomes necessary, and when therefore complicated timetabling decisions need to be made.

With regard to both objections, it depends very much upon the stage of schooling that one is concerned with. At the primary level, for most purposes, the generally educated, intelligent teacher, articulate and widely read in his own language, should have the resources to refine and develop the content and manner of thinking of the pupils who are his responsibility. Weaknesses in particular modes of experience or kinds of performance (in various artistic activities, for instance, or in religious ways of thinking) can be compensated by much greater cooperation between members of staff, and a more open sharing of duties. At the secondary level a reorganisation of the timetable into blocked periods for team teaching in which together the team can draw upon a variety of teaching resources would go some way towards meeting this problem. Such an integration of the curriculum would simply provide the more flexible framework in which a variety of educative resources might be brought into contact with a variety of individual concerns and in which the pupils might gradually be brought to be more reflective, critical, intelligent, disciplined and systematic about the common-sense ways in which they already view themselves, other people, and the world in which they live. Through such a framework, greater demands by the pupil might be made as he becomes preoccupied with questions that demand greater singlemindedness or more disciplined treatment, or as he sees in a teacher a glimpse of a disciplinary ideal, a way of life that has its own attractions. Then, of course, measures need to be taken to ensure this further development of a disciplined mode of enquiry, this further entry into a mode of experiencing. But unless the pupil is so motivated I see little point in forcing such specialised ways of proceeding upon him, i.e. of timetabling him away from what really concerns and interests him.

I believe that many pupils would be better educated (i.e. achieve a more intelligent, able, reflective, critical and extensive capacity to understand their world and to operate in it) if they remained within such an undifferentiated, flexible curriculum framework. I think we deceive ourselves when we think that, by giving many third and fourth formers a complicated timetable, we are initiating them into seven forms of knowledge and innumerable skills. They go through the motions perhaps but they remain basically the same, unaffected in their commonsense view of the world and in their prior attitudes to the 'goodies' which school has had to offer. At best the timetabled subjects become 'commodities' which, like the coins in their pockets, have a certain market value. I spent yesterday helping a third former find his way, via his timetable, to his particular destination in the school. Bewildered by his place amongst the options (needlecraft or woodwork if he had *not* opted to do a second foreign language other than French) and blinded by the many different subjects he was going to 'master', he was being denied the very thing he needed – the ability to seek advice, articulate his problems, describe his bewilderment, gain control over his environment, communicate with his teachers, follow instructions, clarify his own mind about even his simple wants and needs. Despite a lifetime in England and eight years of English schooling he had not yet mastered the English language sufficiently to gain control over his own life, environment, or relationships. The liberal education, the education in breadth, that he was now being subjected to, was for him only an unintelligible ritual. And there are very many like him.

My advocacy therefore of a more integrated curriculum at the earlier stages of secondary schooling rests upon, firstly, a respect for the varied mental activities of the pupils to be educated, secondly, a recognition of the commonsense language and understandings through which the pupils already engage in this mental life and to which the more disciplined modes of enquiry must be related, and thirdly, the need for a more flexible and cooperative teaching framework in which different teacher resources can be brought into contact with so many individual differences. But, as my chapter on the integrated curriculum should have made clear, such a rationale does not support that kind of integrated curriculum in which themes or topics are chosen to be the integrating element. I see no reason why 'dinosaurs', 'communication', or 'survival' should succeed any more than 'history', 'geography' or 'sociology' in bringing the resources of the various public modes of thought and experience to bear upon the active minds of the pupil.

2. Theoretical and practical knowledge

Part of what is meant by 'educating commonsense' is the attempt to get the pupil or student to reflect upon, to look critically at, to make explicit the assumptions of what is already 'known'. The pupil already has a great deal of practical knowledge. He knows *how* to speak, *how* to argue, *how* to find his way about and *how* to relate to various people. He has a great deal of know-how which he can perform more or less well. Part of a teacher's job is of course to extend such know-how so that, for instance, pupils know how to use language more effectively for a greater variety of purposes. Maybe the five-year-old knows how to use language for only a limited number of purposes, for gaining attention or for exercising control over adults, and the teacher's task will be to teach him *how* to use language for other purposes such as describing or clarifying. This will on the whole be achieved by introducing that child into a linguistic community where language has these different functions. Maybe the adolescent boy does not know how to relate easily and confidently to girls, and the most important educational task for him might be to help him gain such practical knowledge. Maybe the university student fails to theorise about structural forces because he does not know how to study – he lacks the practical knowledge which is basic to so much else. Hence a main educational task of the school is to extend the know-how of pupils – the knowledge which enables them to look after themselves and their own interests and to engage fairly independently in the basic activities of a practical life. Such know-how, involving as it does such qualities as self-confidence, commonsense judgement, patience and perseverence, cannot altogether be timetabled or programmed. It is something to be achieved in the living of a practical form of life, and as such ought to be provided by the school when lacking in the home. Part of the educational value of a school – especially a school that mixes abilities, sexes, social classes and races – lies in the practical oppor-

121

tunities provided for learning how to mix socially and to communicate with many different kinds of people. The benefit of many outgoing educational activities – Task Force or community service, for example – lies in the opportunity provided for learning how to accept responsibility for what one does or for initiating and carrying through a scheme of work. One learns to be practical by being practical, and yet this might be the very thing denied to some children.

But extending the know-how is not enough. To reflect upon, to look critically at, to make explicit the hidden assumptions beneath the know-how that the pupil undoubtedly possesses is the beginning of disciplined thinking, of systematic enquiry, indeed of theory. 'Knowing that' is often to put propositionally what previously was only implicit within an often successfully conducted practical life. Its benefit lies in the greater mastery over oneself and one's environment so that one can act more effectively within it and in the capacity for critical reflection that it provides. The theory, the systematic propositional knowledge, which is what so much secondary and higher education is putting across, needs to be rooted in the practical form of life which it is very largely a reflection upon.

If this is the case, constant attention needs to be given to the sort of practical activities which incorporate certain understandings, certain ways of seeing things, which are key ideas in important traditions of disciplined enquiry. The teacher, himself immersed in a particular disciplined mode of thought or enquiry, should recognise those aspects of the pupil's practical know-how which have within them the seeds of much deeper and more extensive understanding. The adolescent conforming to group codes of conduct, responding to particular leaders, taking on particular adolescent roles, constrained by wider social norms and rules, subject to various authorities, relating differently to different social demands, already has an implicit and practical grasp of important sociological truths. He is part of an interesting

122

social community which acts upon him and upon which he acts, but which he very likely cannot reason or talk about because he lacks the concepts, the skills of investigation, the ideas that would make him more aware of, and more able to operate thoughtfully upon, such a social environment. The good teacher of sociology is one who can transform a pupil's or student's consciousness about a social reality which that pupil or student is already immersed in and within which he already has a great deal of practical knowledge. To use the language of Bruner, the teaching requires constant relating of the 'symbolic modes of representation', in which the teacher feels at home and finds understanding, to the 'enactive modes of representation' very often already attained by his pupils. Much teaching must be a constant effort to get the pupil to see the symbolic mode of representing what enactively has been already understood – indeed, not only to see this but also to value it. But often this is not done and theory becomes just a lot of words. Sometimes these words can be memorised with sufficient accuracy and applied with sufficient respect for the logic of the language game for examinations to be passed and certificates won. But their connection with reality – the practical, commonsense reality in which the pupil 'really' operates – is lost. (This is, of course, equally true of so much educational theory.)

3. Breadth and depth

One objection to such a curriculum approach is the lack of coverage that it implies. It will fail to provide examples of, or main structuring ideas within the major intellectual achievements of man. Hirst's argument about seven forms of knowledge was first developed in an article on liberal education. Education is about the development of mind; mind is a mode of consciousness structured by the distinctive conceptual and semantic features of a limited number of forms of knowledge; the proper development of mind therefore lies in the initiation into each of these seven forms. The curriculum conclusion frequently drawn from this is that there should be systematic introduction to subject-matter that reflects the modes of thinking distinctive of each form.

I have challenged this view, especially in chapter 2 but implicitly throughout the book. Firstly, the children already have a very active mental life long before they come in contact with organised programmes of teaching. This complex and frequently very sophisticated commonsense world children inhabit must either itself contain the differentiated consciousness that Hirst is so keen upon (in which case they will require no initiation) or must in no way characterise the life of *mind*. But this of course would be absurd. Secondly, I argued that the case for such a reduced set of categories of thought was itself untenable. Man's achievement lies in an evermore differentiated mode of enquiry and experience, in a more differentiated set of performances and strivings. These are by no means so few as seven in number. Nor are such acheivements (cognitive though they be) all of truth seeking, theoretical kinds. Hence the range of possible subject-matters upon which the curriculum might draw is indefinite; the possible traditions of thought and enquiry in which the teacher might find his teaching resources are innumerable, and the process of selection, the decision about sufficient breadth, cannot be assisted by any reduction of all this to a few fundamental forms or categories.

Thirdly, however, I argued that one could reasonably talk about qualities and powers of the mind independently of particular modes of mental activity, even though their exercise or their development might be impossible except within or through a particular mode of mental life. It makes sense to talk about people being in general intelligent, creative, reflective, analytic, judicious, imaginative, thoughtful, sensitive and so on. Indeed there is a tradition within the Civil Service that the administrator should have acquired such qualities (whether as a result of studying classics, history,

124

sociology does not matter) and should apply them to various practical and administrative problems without necessarily any profound knowledge of the particular content of what he is administering. What are the professional advisers for, if not for that? The well trained mind is one that can turn itself to a multitude of theoretical and practical problems because, in its training, it has gained certain qualities and powers of mind even if the particular content through which these have been gained has now been forgotten.

With these fourth formers the main task of the teacher would be to help them to be more intelligent, judicious, sensitive, imaginative about the commonsense thinking and ways of acting that they were already engaged in. They, like anyone else, needed to acquire greater powers of reflecting, of analysing, of disciplining their enquiries, of relating conclusions to evidence. Such abilities required qualities of a quasimoral kind, intellectual virtues if you like: perseverence with a task, concern for the true or correct answer, openness to criticism. Some of their interests and concerns might not give too much scope for the exercise of the mind, for disciplining the intellect or opening up the imagination, and the task of the teacher would then be to help identify those interests and concerns that had such a scope. Indeed one would rarely have far to look. The most disruptive and threatening member of my class was almost completely self-taught in electronics. His passion for this mode of understanding, unrecognised by the school, had landed him in court several times. And his inability to further this interest either at school or at nightschool (impossible until he had left fulltime schooling) alienated him from what the school offered instead. And yet the study of electronic systems, the mastery of their intricate detail and the principles that lay behind their use, was as demanding and satisfying an intellectual task as any other.

I see no basis therefore for selecting from the many achievements of mankind, from the very many accessible traditions of enquiry and experiencing, any particular few as paradigm cases of what it means to have a mind. The principle of selection cannot be found in any *a priori* examination of what it means to have a mind or what it is to know that something is the case, but only in attending to the particular interests and concerns of those very people one is seeking to educate. Of course, in attending to such interests and concerns, in helping the child to be more intelligent, judicious, sensitive, imaginative, about what he is interested in, the teacher will draw upon such accessible traditions of thought and experience, and indeed the value and the validity of such traditions lies partly in the contribution they can make to the commonsense questionings and strivings of such pupils. This is no way detracts from the argument that, since it is these pupils' minds that are to be developed, it is to the preoccupations and current modes of thinking of such minds that we must turn in deciding what needs to be selected in assisting *their* mental development.

4. Development: internal and external norms

My main objection to so much curriculum practice is the lack of respect for the *development* of the pupil's mind, and this lack of respect has found support in a theory of education which stresses *initiation* into forms of knowledge. The assumption is that there is a distinction in kind between the understandings brought to the school (or to the college or to the university) by the learner, which can be discounted as of not much worth, and the understandings revealed by the different subjects on the curriculum. But I have objected to that on two counts. In the first place, the understandings brought to the school not only serve the learner well for a large number of purposes but they (unless they receive sympathetic but critical attention of the educator) will remain untouched by the school and will remain the dominant influence in how the pupil continues to think, feel, and approach life's problems.

126

Secondly, the different modes of enquiry are themselves rooted in commonsense thinking; they have themselves developed from systematic and cooperative reflection upon a mode of consciousness that originally was not particularly systematic or reflective. And unless connections can be made between the respected, academic and disciplined modes of enquiry and this mode of consciousness – often inadequate, often unsystematic and unreflective – of the learner, then the point and the validity of their subject-matters, incorporated into the syllabus, will be lost. If connections are not made wherein lies the education?

To develop the mind, therefore, requires attending to the individual's mind, to the particular concepts and principles, to the particular skills of enquiry, to the kinds of feeling response that characterises his conscious life. Such attention will reveal where concepts need refining, where distinctions need to be made, where the conceptual structuring of the speech or activity is inadequate for the intended purpose. An infant cannot make his wishes known because words are lacking. In mastering a word he is refining a concept, developing a more adequate, sharper classification of events.

It is such characteristics of development – the gradual change and refinement of the conceptual apparatus that is already there and that is constantly found to be inadequate for particular purposes or in particular 'conversations' – that has led some educational philosophers in the past to compare educational growth to the growth of a plant. The child is like a plant to be watered, fertilised, repotted, or simply allowed to grow. Or it has led more recently to talk about 'personal adjustment' or 'negotiation of meanings' or to 'reconstruction of different realities'.

This however is to ignore the external norm of development. Not any kind of adjustment, or negotiation or reconstruction will do. The different modes of understanding, the different ways of behaving and of enquiring, upon which the teacher draws, contain criteria of worth, of

127

correctness, of truth to which any genuine development of thought must submit. That these, though socially developed and legitimated by social acclaim, are not *just* conventional and are not arbitrary or open to individual choice, was the main force of my argument in chapter 4. Hence, respect for the commonsense understandings of the pupil – the refinement and development of these – by no means signifies disrespect for objective and defensible standards. These are to be located in and made accessible through the different publicly developed traditions of thought, enquiry and feeling, and must be brought to bear upon the thoughts, enquiries and feelings of the pupil by teachers immersed in these traditions.

References and Name index

ARCHAMBAULT, R. D. (1956) The philosophical basis of the experience curriculum. *Harvard Educational Review,* **26** No 3. *66*

BERNSTEIN, B. (1967) Open schools, open society. *New Society,* 14 April 1967. *104*

BERNSTEIN, B. (1971) On the classification and framing of educational knowledge. In Young (1971). *72*

BRUNER, J. S. (1960) *The Process of Education.* Cambridge, Mass., Harvard U.P. *29, 46*

BRUNER, J. S. (1966) *Towards a Theory of Instruction.* Cambridge, Mass., Harvard U.P. *24*

COLLINGS, E. (1923) *An Experiment with a Project Curriculum.* New York, Macmillan. *47*

DEWEY, J. (1916) *Democracy and Education.* New York, Macmillan. *2, 23, 52, 56, 59, 66, 98*

DEWEY, J. (1933) *How we Think.* Revised ed., Boston, Heath. *58*

DEWEY, J. (1938) *Experience and Education.* London, Collier-Macmillan. *59, 66*

FILMER, P. and others (1972) *New Directions in Sociological Theory.* London, Collier-Macmillan. *83*

FORD, G. W. and PUGNO, L. (1964) *The Structure of Knowledge and the Curriculum.* Chicago, Rand McNally. *46*

GOLDSMITH'S COLLEGE CURRICULUM LABORATORY (1969) Report No 6, London. *57, 60*

GORBUTT, D., BOWDEN, T. and PRING, R. A. (1972) Education as the control of knowledge. *Education for Teaching*, **89**. *67, 83*

HAMLYN, D. W. (1970) *The Theory of Knowledge*. London, Macmillan. *23*

HIRST, P. H. (1965) Liberal education and the nature of knowledge. In Archambault, R. D., *Philosophical Analysis and Education*. London, Routledge and Kegan Paul. *37ff., 42, 43, 46*

HIRST, P. H. (1973) Literature and the fine arts as a unique form of knowledge. *Cambridge Journal of Education*, **3** No 3. *43*

HIRST, P. H. (1974) *Knowledge and the Curriculum*. London, Routledge and Kegan Paul. *46*

HIRST, P. H. and PETERS, R. S. (1970) *The Logic of Education*. London, Routledge and Kegan Paul. *40*

JAMES, C. (1968) *Young Lives at Stake*. London, Collins. *58, 114*

KEELE INTEGRATED STUDIES TEAM (1972) *Exploration Man: an Introduction to Integrated Studies*. O.U.P. *105*

KILPATRICK, W. H. (1918) *The Project Method*. New York, Teachers' College of Columbia University. *2, 48, 51, 52, 56, 59*

KUHN, T. S. (1962) *The Structure of Scientific Revolutions*. University of Chicago Press. *78*

MILL, J. S. (1863) *Utilitarianism*. London, Dent. *54*

PERRY, L. R. (1965) Commonsense thought, knowledge and judgement, and their importance for education. *British Journal of Educational studies*, **13** No 2. *98*

PETERS, R. S. (1966) *Ethics and Education*. London, Allen and Unwin. *23, 85*

PETERS, R. S. (1967) In defence of bingo: a rejoinder. *British Journal of Educational Studies*, **15** No 2. *54*

PHENIX, P. H. (1964) *Realms of Meaning*. New York, McGraw Hill. *35f., 42, 46*

PRING, R. A. (1971) Curriculum integration. *Proceedings of the Philosophy of Education Society of Great Britain*, **5** No 2. *114*

PRING, R. A. (1976) See The Open University (1976). *46, 103, 104, 114*

REID, L. A. (1961) *Ways of Knowledge and Experience*. London, Allen and Unwin. *46*

REID, L. A. (1974) The arts as a unique form of knowledge. *Cambridge Journal of Education*, **4** No 3. *45*

RYLE, G. (1949) *The Concept of Mind*. London, Hutchinson. *24*

SCHEFFLER, I. (1965) *Conditions of Knowledge*. Chicago, Scott Foresman. *24*

SCHWAB, J. J. (1964) Structure of the disciplines: meanings and significance. In Ford and Pugno (1964). *46*

SCHWAB, J. J. (1969) *College Curriculum and Student Protest*. University of Chicago Press. *46*

SCRIMSHAW, P. (1973) Statements, language and art: some comments on professor Hirst's paper. *Cambridge Journal of Education*, **3** No 3. *44*

STENHOUSE, L. (1968) The humanities curriculum project. *Journal of Curriculum Studies*, **1** No 3. *108*

THE OPEN UNIVERSITY (1976) E203 *Curriculum Design and Development*, Unit 11 *Subjects, Activities, Themes, Cores* and Unit 12 *The Integrated Curriculum*. Milton Keynes, The Open University Press. [By R. A. Pring.]

WALTON, J. (1971) (ed.) *The Integrated Day in Theory and Practice*. London, Ward Lock. *114*

WARWICK, D. (1973) (ed.) *Integrated Studies in the Secondary School*. University of London Press. *114*

WHITE, A. R. (1967) *The Philosophy of Mind*. New York, Random House. *24*

WHITEHEAD, A. N. (1932) *The Aims of Education*. London, Benn. *98*

WHITTY, G. (1974) Sociology and the problem of radical educational change. In Flude, M. and Ahier, J. (eds.) *Educability in Schools and Ideology*. London, Croom Helm. *70, 83*

WILSON, P. S. (1967) In defence of bingo. *British Journal of Educational Studies*, **15** No 1. *52, 54*

WILSON, P. S. (1971) *Interest and Discipline in Education*. London, Routledge and Kegan Paul. *52, 53, 54, 66*

YOUNG, M. F. D. (1971) (ed.) *Knowledge and Control*. London, Collier-Macmillan. *83*

Subject index